Girl Talk...
God Talk

SALLY MILLER

HARVEST HOUSE PUBLISHERS

EUGENE, OREGON

Cover by Garborg Design Works, Minneapolis, Minnesota

GIRL TALK...GOD TALK
Copyright © 2006 by Sally Miller
Published by Harvest House Publishers
Eugene, Oregon 97402
www.harvesthousepublishers.com

Library of Congress Cataloging-in-Publication Data

Miller, Sally, 1968-
Girl talk...God talk / Sally Miller.
   p. cm.
Includes bibliographical references.
ISBN-13: 978-0-7369-1693-6 (pbk.)
ISBN-10: 0-7369-1693-8
1. Christian women—Religious life. 2. Female friendship—Religious aspects—Christianity. I. Title.
   BV4527.M47 2006
   248.8'43—dc22   2005019221

Printed in the United States of America

06 07 08 09 10 11 12 13 14 /DP-KB/ 10 9 8 7 6 5 4 3 2 1

*For my friends from
Wheaton and beyond.*

Acknowledgments

First and foremost, I would like to thank the girlfriends who walk with me in ways that help me see and know God.

To Cheri for being midwife, editor, and companion to a sometimes misguided bird; to Margie for making crepes and strong Brazilian coffee; to Heather, Beth, and Jules who prayed "softly at night, boldly in the shower, and with each lighting cardinal"; and to Laura for postpartum editorial comments and encouragement.

A special thank-you to Rob for being my "agent," brother, and friend. Your insights into my writing and life come from propinquity at its best! I love you and Kristin, my sister-in-love-to-be!

And to my publisher, Terry Glaspey. You took the two-by-fours of *Girl Talk* and provided the blueprint needed to build a book. You are brilliant!

This book would have remained treasured memories were it not for Barbara Gordon, my editor, Betty, Barb, Carolyn, Paul, and others at Harvest House who nurtured this self-taught writer with grace and professional integrity.

To those at Blanchard Road, especially Ken and Tina, Anna and Scott, Donna, Lisa, and Mark. I am indebted to each of you for your bolstering and prayers.

My gratitude goes out to everyone in my family for their support, especially Mom and Dad, who took the boys to the park and kept them happy with trips to Oberweis while I nested in my writing room.

And to Bryan, whom I adore. You are much more to me than tech support. You are my second favorite carpenter...and the love of my life!

For giving what follows, I'd like to thank God, by whose grace, wildness, and wisdom I've learned many things, not the least of which is that all of life is prayer.

Contents

Always stay connected to people and seek out things that bring you joy. Dream with abandon. Pray confidently.

—BARBARA JOHNSON

Why Did Prayer Feel Like Drudgery?

Come if you're thirsty, or weak,
or if you carry a heavy burden.
Come when you're jumping for joy or
when you're yearning to be near God.
Come if you're ripe with years or
if you're just beginning life's journey.
Come if you're alone or with a community of friends.
Come as you are.
Come and pray.

MATTHEW 11:28 (paraphrased)

Racing 'Round the Rosary

For as long as I can remember, I've wanted to talk with God. Many nights, as a ten-year-old girl, I'd grit my teeth and promise, *God, I will pray this entire set of prayer beads before I fall asleep.* That old set of beads now hangs on my closet doorknob, an icon for the beginning of my prayer journey.

The beads were actually a rosary given to me by a family friend, Anita. She dutifully taught me how to say each "Glory Be" and "Our Father" from the Catholic faith. And I practiced them to perfection. The string of beads enchanted me. I thought it was my ticket to closeness with God, a certificate of spiritual sanctity. The fact that the beads were grape-sized and glow-in-the-dark added to the charm.

Before bed, I'd gather them in my hands, holding them up to the light on my nightstand. I'd count to 50 or wait until my palms started to sweat. Then I'd know that the white pearls were recharged with luminescence. Into my bed I'd burrow, all the way to the foot, under a glowing tent of sheets.

Our Father, Who art in Heaven, hallowed be Thy Name… I'd begin, as I rolled one of the plastic pearls between my thumb and index finger. During the first few recitations, I'd try to focus on the meaning of the words. But after the fourth "Our Father," I'd begin to rush, running words and phrases together in hopes of rounding the beaded bend, making it to the crucifix dangling dozens of prayers away.

Within ten minutes, my breath would inevitably slow, getting deeper. My eyelids would become heavy under the weight of sleepiness. And my grip on the beads would loosen. They'd slide out of my hand and off my mattress, landing on the floor like a bag of loose marbles, ricocheting into a ragged round.

In the morning, I'd awaken feeling guilty, undisciplined, and unspiritual.

The Quixotic Quest for Quiet Times

Years later my longing to talk with God remained. Pam, a friend and mentor, taught me about "quiet times": moments in the morning set aside to "meet with God." Taking her advice, I set my alarm clock for 5:30 each morning. Unfortunately, I had a chronic snooze button habit that still plagues me today.

Discouraged, I talked to Pam again. This time she gave me an acronym for P.R.A.Y.: P=praise, R=repentance, A=ask (for others), and Y=yourself. She told me I could pray *any* time during the day (not just in the mornings and evenings when I was the sleepiest).

Having a format helped. Knowing that I could pray in the car, at the mall, and during my afternoon jog helped, too. After using P.R.A.Y. for a few years, I became free enough within the structure to realize some comfort in my conversations with God.

An Unexpected Epiphany

At the same time, I'll admit that I was dumbfounded when I overheard people lauding the "joys of prayer life." My prayer experience felt more like an obligatory, grin-and-bear-it exercise. It seemed like dull, dark drudgery of sweat and will. I constantly felt guilty about not praying enough or in the right ways. I wondered why I was missing the breadth, color, and vitality others seemed to find in their conversations with God.

As strange as it may sound, I'm thankful for the years of beaded prayers, sleepy quiet times, and conversational acronyms. They didn't slake my thirst for God. Instead, they prepared my palate for the fullness found in *life as prayer*. They whetted my appetite for the freedom, intimacy, and imagination possible in talks with God. They nudged me to consider a broader definition of prayer, and then find it explained through an unexpected place: my girlfriends.

What My Girlfriends Taught Me About Prayer

Prayers are as simple as talking and listening to a friend. In his letter to the Thessalonians, Paul writes, "pray continually, or without ceasing." Knowing we have children to raise, sunsets to watch, races to run, dishes to wash, and paintings to paint, it's obvious that Paul has a broad definition of prayer in mind. He's not suggesting we become spiritual Cinderellas—swept up in a magic ball of heavenly holiness. Instead, he's acknowledging our down-to-earth lives. His "pray without ceasing" means prayer is as simple and daily as life itself.

With our girlfriends, we take walks communicating without words, chatter and giggle into the middle of the night, cry and silently hug, or linger over cups of tea. Our very being, breath, and movement with them is a kind of connection. We live our lives together. Because of close, messy, lovely, real, intimate relationships with friends, I've discovered that prayer is simple, divine, and daily. It's more than a conversation. It's a *relationship*.

Our relationship with God changes with circumstances, times, moods, and days. There are seasons of drought and seasons of plenty in our prayer lives. We don't have to worry if a day or two goes by and we don't talk to God. Sometimes silence can be a prayer. God knows our hearts. Every day, no matter what, He is with us. If we remember that, our definition of prayer broadens.

My friends give me gifts on my birthdays. They tell me when a pair of jeans makes my butt look as big as the whale that swallowed Jonah. I laugh hysterically because of their off-center jokes. They know everything about me, from my favorite flavor of ice cream (chocolate peanut butter) to the deepest dreams and desires of my heart. And they cry when I cry. Knowing how my girlfriends relate to me helps open my heart to an intimate, playful, ongoing interaction with God. Because of my friends, I catch fresh glimpses of Him. *God calls me on the phone to have a simple chat. He takes a walk with me. He sits next to me on the couch. He does a dance of joy. He whispers in my ear.*

Maybe these scenarios sound strange or irreverent to you. Maybe it seems weird comparing a relationship with God to the relationships between giggly, imperfect, and sometimes catty girlfriends. But Jesus was best friends with a crew of stinky fishermen who probably used language that'd make Eddie Murphy look like the pope. Jesus knows what it feels like to wear skin, be betrayed by a friend, walk on dusty streets, and get sand between his toes. He's like us, and we're like Him. We're created "in His image" (Genesis 1:27). Because of this, we can relate to God through each other.

In fact, *people* are our best bet at knowing God. The unthinkable fact that the God of the universe somehow fit into a manger is reason enough to believe that we can find Christ in our friends. Our close girlfriends show us many of the ways we can be in a prayerful relationship with Jesus. They help us see who God *really* is: Initiator, Savior, Host, Playmate, Redeemer, Artist, and Friend.

Girl Talk...God Talk explores a myriad of stories about friends who shed light on the qualities of God's person and, ultimately, on prayer. Each chapter is divided into three sections:

> *Girl Talk:* A story about a friend
> *God Talk:* How God is revealed in the story
> *Walking the Talk:* How this truth about God fits into our lives

Seeing God through the window of friendship opens our hearts to God's deep love. We see His involvement in our everyday lives. Our prayer horizon is broadened to a vast, wide, organic, imaginative, and daily fullness. And we are

encouraged to embrace a full, rich, prayer life replete with
revelation and relationship.

*Our thinking about prayer, whether right or wrong,
is based on our own mental conception of it. The correct
concept is to think of prayer as the breath in our lungs and
the blood from our hearts. Our blood flows and our
breathing continues "without ceasing"; we are not even
conscious of it, but it never stops….Prayer is not an
exercise, it is the life of the saint.*[1]

OSWALD CHAMBERS

1

The Heart of Hospitality

A Welcome to Prayer

*Friends give nourishment of all kinds to one
another. We sustain one another. In so
many ways we offer to one another the
feasts of our friendship.*[1]

MADELEINE L'ENGLE

Girl Talk—Margaret's Table

Everyone needs a friend who has the heart of a hostess: someone like Margaret. She finds pleasure in setting a table, making a meal, and celebrating life's landmarks. Sometimes she serves up simple bowls of soup with sourdough. Other times she creates gourmet meals of Beef Wellington and Profiteroles. Either way, her welcoming heart is what matters most.

Last fall, Margaret invited me over for a birthday brunch. I had a 2000-word article about adoption due the next day. My oldest son was sick. The car needed gas. And my laundry sat in mounds bigger than Everest on my family room floor. I had too many obligations to spend a leisurely day with friends.

But I went any way. On my walk to her front door, autumn leaves—golden, orange, and crimson—descended like manna. I hardly noticed their beauty. Instead, I repeatedly ruminated over the section headers for my article: *Adoption, Enlarging Hearts & Homes, The Gift of a Daughter, Replacing Fear with Faith.* They echoed like a skipping CD over and over in my subconscious.

Margaret greeted me at the door with a warm hug and a whispered, "Happy birthday, Sally." I hardly heard her. But I found myself drawn in by the smell of my favorite coffee brewing on the stove. It was pumpkin and spice. When Margaret poured me a cup and offered me a seat, worries about work waned for the first time all day.

Three of my other friends showed up, and Margaret invited them in. Everyone set down festive birthday packages as they oohed and aahed over Margaret's beautifully decorated table. It was set with colorful plates, napkins folded into hearts, and a centerpiece of bright sunflowers. Nestled in the middle of a sage-colored tablecloth was Margaret's famous frittata. She served heaping helpings of her savory concoction and poured more smooth, dark coffee. Moment by moment my tension began to melt like the butter on Margaret's freshly baked bread.

My girlfriends and I feasted. Conversation flowed and laughter followed. Cheri launched in with alarming news that she'd already finished her Christmas shopping. Hannah followed with a joke. She mentioned that God should've sent wise *women* to Bethlehem. *Women* would have "used MapQuest, arrived punctually, been midwives, sanitized the stable, made chicken soup, and brought shower gifts," she said.

Smirks aside, everyone agreed that the joke would have some validity if God had sent someone like Margaret. She would have thought of every detail for welcoming Jesus into the world with warmth and wonder. Clearly, she'd have brought gifts more practical than gold, frankincense, and myrrh, such as a baby quilt for the manger, a postpartum shower gel for Mary, or a flashlight to light the stable.

I know that Margaret would have celebrated Jesus' birth with fervor because of the way she celebrated mine—with a magnificent meal, balloons hovering above my chair, her beautiful table, and the candle that flickered by my place setting. Because of Margaret's knack for creating a cozy environment, I know I am loved, accepted, and celebrated. She helps lift my worries. She fills my stomach as well as my soul. And she gives me little glimpses of God, our divine host.

Around the table we sit, as the candles flicker and burn down. We share ideas. We share food. We share our sense of calling, affirming again that we are here to do God's will and praying we will be given the grace to discern what God's will is. Lamb and potatoes. Bread and wine. Enjoyed together, in the understanding that all of life is a sacrament.[2]

MADELEINE L'ENGLE

God Talk—A Divine Banquet Table

Knowing firsthand what it feels like to receive Margaret's hospitality, I feel awed and overwhelmed imagining God as my host. But He is. In fact, He beckons all of us to "come to the table." Sometimes, it's difficult to picture a powerful, omnipotent God as host. It's baffling that He wants to serve and sup with people like us: traitors, prostitutes, tax collectors, and those who deny knowing Him (John 18:15-18,25-27; Mark 2:16). Picture the scene. There's an oak table decked in white linen and topped with hundreds of candles glowing in enormous golden candelabras. Platters overflow with fruit and meats. Baskets brim with bread. God has a waiter's towel draped over His left arm. He's ready to take orders and open a bottle of Merlot (Luke 12:37).

At His table, many are seated. In a row are the Menendez brothers, Mother Teresa, the Long Island Lolita, Pete Rose, Saddam Hussein, Gandhi, Hillary Clinton, Princess Diana, Jeffrey Dahmer, and me. Shocking picture, isn't it? Maybe the most shocking part of all is that *I'm* included.

This image is uncomfortable. It causes me to judge others, even God, and then myself. *Why is he or she here? God, You sure are generous and indiscriminate with your invitations. Why am I here, if I'm asking these kinds of questions? Maybe I don't "deserve" to be at Your table like I thought I did.*

After a while, I recognize the circuitous nature of my ponderings. Trying to slow the flow of condemnation, I take my focus off of the flaws of others and my own inadequacies. Instead I try to look at the facts. God's banquet is plenteous and beautiful. The table is long. There are many seats. His heart is loving, gentle, open.

"You prepare a table before me" (Psalm 23:5).

God's divine welcome is comparable to the brunch Margaret planned for my birthday. She wanted to celebrate my life and be close to me as a friend. Uncannily, God feels the same way. Even though I've gained ten pounds since my last birthday, forgot to bring treats for my son's preschool on Wednesday, and lied in order to get a free parking voucher in Chinatown, God still invites me to come to His table. He welcomes me to a life of prayerful communion. He sees the imaginary sticker I have stuck to my forehead that reads in red: *AS IS*. And He wants me anyway.

Whenever I think I don't deserve to be close to God, I listen to a song by Michael Card called "Come to the Table." In it, Michael sings of a feast including the "bread of forgiveness," and the sweet "wine of release." He tells the story of sitting beside Christ and seeing the look of forgiveness and love in His eyes. It's a look forsaking condemnation, offering pardon and peace.

When I hear afresh about God's love, it gives me a yearning to pray. It compels me to connect with Him—but not out of guilt or shame or obligation. His invitation, sealed with love, induces me to gratefulness and makes me hunger for the feast.

Instead of counting on myself to muscle through a life of prayer, I realize that God longs for us to meet. He actually prepares for our connections, metaphorically cooking, cleaning, and decorating. All I have to do is show up. He's the one who makes a life of prayer plausible, even possible.

God initiates conversations with me and responds to my prayers 24-7. His banqueting table is set for me wherever I go. Sometimes I find His feast at church, other times it's at playground picnics, or at fiestas for 50. He prepares the same abundant feast even during little luncheons for two. God is waiting in all the nooks and crannies of my life. He sets a place for me while I scrub floors, drive my boys to preschool, take my afternoon walk, and lay my head on my pillow each night. He's available when I need Him. He speaks words of encouragement, help, hope, and even humor when I need them the most.

Because of Margaret's example, I know God wants to commune with me. He wants to hear my requests and fears, worries and thanksgivings, angers and hopes. And He wants to speak words of love and grace into my life. Out of gratitude, I figuratively polish my silver, set out sparkling goblets, and make a magnificent meal. As I do, I set the table of my heart for Him.

Walking the Talk

1. How have you received God's invitation to a life of prayer? Make a list of ways He is welcoming you.

2. Read the following poem. If you choose, make it your heart's prayer this week. Maybe it will inspire you to write a poem of welcome to God or a friend this week.

Choreo (Come, Lord Jesus)
by Sally Miller

I welcome you
    to my messy family room
    toys on the carpet
    fire lit

> I welcome you
>> into my broken body
>> aching and worn
>> heart soft
>
> I welcome you
>> into my cluttered mind
>> spinning, frenetic, and full
>> wanting a word from you
>
> I welcome you
>> into my soul
>> anxious and alone
>> needing holy companionship

3. Make a meal for a friend who has just given birth. The dinner is a small way to lighten her load during a hectic season and to welcome her as she's initiated into motherhood.

4. Set your table. If you are a hostess-type like Margaret, gather a group of friends and welcome them through your gracious hospitality. Think about the ways God wants to welcome you to a prayerful life.

He has taken me to the banquet hall,
and his banner over me is love.

SONG OF SONGS 2:4

Lord, thank You for friends who grace me with their hospitality. Thanks also for the ways You are host, welcoming me to a prayerful life. May I accept the invitation…and extend a welcome to You in return. Amen.

2
Known...and Loved Nonetheless

Freedom for Embarrassment During Prayer

Love covers over all wrongs.

PROVERBS 10:12

Girl Talk—Hannah's Phone Call

Multitasking. It's the way lawyers effectively serve their clients, writers meet deadlines, carpenters build houses, and homemakers survive. In my circle of friends, including the women at Margaret's birthday brunch, many are master multitaskers. Over the years they've successfully shown me that boiling water for spaghetti, cleaning the kitchen floor, and quizzing children for upcoming spelling bees can be done simultaneously.

I'm actually multitasking right now. While I type I'm waiting for my sons to finish breakfast, doing laundry (it's clearly on an unbalanced spin cycle), and listening to my favorite CD (a mix of Mozart greats). Usually the benefits of doing several things at the same time outweigh the costs. The other day, however, I wondered if multitasking was as wonderful as it's cracked up to be.

It was only 7:30 in the morning, and the day was flurrying with as much activity as the atmosphere was with snow. I had laundry waiting to be folded in the family room, the boys were getting dressed for preschool in their bedroom, a phone was ringing in the kitchen, and my bladder was warning me about an overdue appointment with the bathroom. Hoping that the magical powers of multitasking would save me, I took the phone into the powder room.

It was Hannah, my friend and fellow Wheaton College grad. We were trying to make arrangements to bring a meal for a girlfriend who had just given birth. "I'll bring crudités, brownies, and something...a bottle of Merlot," she said. "Do you want to bring a green salad and a..." While Hannah was finishing her sentence, my three-year-old, Ayden, walked into the bathroom. His pants were on backward, pockets flying from hips like flags. His rugby shirt was inside out. It randomly framed his porcupine hairdo.

Ayden had dressed himself, and I was proud of him. My smile was natural and grateful, an ornament for the nod of appreciation I tossed in his direction. He smiled back at me. Then he approached, loudly asking, "Mama, can I see your potty when you're done?" His tiny tenor ricocheted off the bathroom walls straight into the phone receiver.

I was mortified! An elevator of heat rose from my chin, up my face, and through my scalp. Uncomfortable silence hung like a vapor. Then Hannah intervened with hearty, familiar, gut-deep giggles. "So you're multitasking again?" she asked rhetorically while she roared. Honestly and warmly Hannah lightened the moment with knowing laughter and love.

Clearly *that* was not the most embarrassing moment I've shared with Hannah. She was at the ladies luncheon where I spoke for an hour with a large piece of lettuce lodged between my incisors. (After the conference, I asked her why she kept on pointing to her teeth with an anxious, compulsive twitch. Now I know why!) On another occasion, she was helping me lead worship at a local church when I tripped over a mic cord, and broke my little finger after falling down two steps. (And the stories could go on and on...)

Sharing embarrassing moments is part of the tangle of friendship. Close friends are bound to know our weaknesses and foibles. I'm just glad that friends like Hannah, who *really* know me, still choose to love me.

It may sound strange, but sometimes our idiosyncrasies actually endear our friends to us. All of my girlfriends know I'm olympically uncoordinated, have a weakness for all things sparkly, am prone to hyperbole, and that I can be extremely insecure underneath a façade of confidence. Instead of judging me and discarding my friendship because I'm a little rough around the edges, they laugh at my quirks and eccentricities and love me just the same.

Their acceptance frees me to be the imperfect, immature mortal that I am. It helps me assuage the guilt and shame I feel when I make a mistake or don't seem to measure up. On an even deeper level, my friends forgive me and walk with me as I work through my most base faults, shortcomings, and vices such as greediness, jealousy, comparison, and covetousness.

Stepping into the fray of friendship—being really known—can be scary, even with friends as gracious as Hannah. It's worth it though because there's nothing on earth as good as being known...and loved nonetheless.

There are friends who are forever part of you and your journey. Those you can cry with, sharing griefs and faults. Those you can laugh with, free and joyful as small children in uninhibited mirth....Those you can pray with on the deepest level, exposing yourselves totally to God's love.[1]

MADELEINE L'ENGLE

God Talk — A Comfortable Connection

O LORD, you have searched me and you know me. You know when I sit and when I rise; you perceive my thoughts from afar. You discern my going out and my lying down; you are familiar with all my ways. Before a word is on my tongue you know it completely, O LORD.

PSALM 139:1-4

Being known, loved, and accepted by our friends is a perfect mirror of God's love for us. And while our friends may know us quite well, no one knows us like God does. "Man looks at the outward appearance, but the LORD looks at the heart" (1 Samuel 16:7). *Wow!* It feels vulnerable being known by girlfriends. So God's X-ray kind of knowing seems a little *too* close for comfort.

He knows us as well as a physician knows anatomy. He's our Maker. The psalmist agrees: "For you created my inmost being; you knit me together in my mother's womb....My frame was not hidden from you when I was made in the secret place. When I was woven together in the depths of the earth, your eyes saw my unformed body" (Psalm 139:13,15-16). God sees and knows all of our parts, healthy and human, beautiful and broken, wonderful and wicked.

To top it off, He's *with* us all of the time. God thoughtfully chose the name for His only Son: Emmanuel. It means *God with us*...God with me: before, behind, beside, even inside. Clearly, there's no way to hide my warts, insufficiencies, and scars from Him. He sees them all and "knows me full well." (I can't even go into the bathroom to hide from God.)

This total revealing used to make me nervous, even itchy. It bothered me to think that God always knew where I was, what I was doing, even what I was thinking. I found His presence more terrifying than comforting. Feelings of embarrassment and shame plagued me. It freaked me out to merely live my life, not to mention actually *talking* to this God who knew me so well.

Unfortunately, I think I was fearful of God because of my misconstrued image of Him. It's strange to admit, but for years I pictured God as a cross between an angry father and a deified version of Santa Claus. (Keep in mind that I believe in the value of myth and enjoy reading *'Twas the Night Before Christmas* to my boys on Christmas Eve each year.) However, the words from *Santa Claus Is Comin' to Town* didn't necessarily prove to be a positive contribution to my spiritual formation.

The whole "better watch out" thing really scared me. The idea of Santa seeing me when I was sleeping and knowing when I was awake was quite bothersome. All of this led to my tramatic perception of God as a watchman making notes in a "naughty or nice notebook."

Keeping this in mind today, I try to celebrate the myth of Santa with my kids in a little more sensitive manner. I know I can't get away from the song. (It's fun and a classic. The kids love to sing it, and so do I!) But instead of portraying a Grinch of a God, I try to focus on the benevolent, gracious, fatherly love of an omnipotent Santa; the kind of love that Hannah helped me discover. Wondrously, this treatment of Santa has poured over into my spiritual life (and into my kids', too).

No matter what paradigm we espouse as we perceive God, it can be healthy to examine it. One of the best ways of doing this is imagining how a true friend would be. All of the gifts found in friendship: grace, love, acceptance, admonition, patience, lightheartedness, faithfulness, kindness, gentleness, and goodness can be found multiplied exponentially in God.

With my old perceptions of God, the place of prayer felt more like sitting in a metal folding chair behind a lie-detector test than in an inviting, cozy, overstuffed chair visiting with someone who loves me. I wondered: *Would I offend God? Would I say too much? Not enough? Were there certain things I should or should not pray about? Would I sound stupid and insignificant to the God who "hung the stars in place" and knows the secrets of the universe? And what is He thinking when He sees all the creepy cobwebbed corners of my life and soul?*

When questions like those swirl in my brain and fears mount like the dishes in my kitchen sink, it helps to remember the cushiony feeling of Hannah's laughter and loving acceptance. It's good to recall the safety I sense in her steadfast, full-knowing kind of connection. It makes room for me to feel in awe of God, but at the same time to not be afraid of Him. It helps me realize that His love is liberating.

He applauds all of our movements toward Him. He celebrates the times we find Him because He always finds us. Even though we may feel like we're only a lost penny, He regards us as a lost treasure (Luke 15:9). Our value to Him does not diminish because of limps, stutters, impairments, or imperfections. He wants us to come—just as we are—to pray.

The good news is that God loves and wants all of us, at our best and worst, because it is out of this extraordinary mixture that God weaves the warp and woof of our souls.[2]

MADELEINE L'ENGLE

Walking the Talk

You created my inmost being; you knit me together in my mother's womb...My frame was not hidden from you when I was made in the secret place.

PSALM 139:13,15

1. Think of a friend who knows you well and loves you anyway. Write her a note and thank her for showing Christ's kind of love to you.

2. Is there anything you've been trying to hide from God? How does it make you feel to realize that He already knows your "little secret" and loves you anyway? Write or think about it. Tell God a secret that you'd normally only share with your closest friend. How does it make you feel? Isn't it freeing to be honest with yourself and with God?

> *Lord, thank You for knowing me inside out and loving me anyway. Remove my fear, unnecessary embarrassment, and shame. Help me see myself and others with Your eyes of love. Amen.*

Long-Distance Friendship?

Prayer as Everyday and Everywhere

> *Friendship is the greatest of worldly goods.*
> *Certainly to me it is the chief happiness of*
> *life. If I had to give a piece of advice to a*
> *young man about a place to live, I think I*
> *[should] say, "sacrifice almost everything to*
> *live where you can be near your friends."*[1]
>
> C.S. LEWIS

Girl Talk—Cheri, My Close–Faraway Friend

Cheri is so much a part of my life I sometimes feel that she's a sister rather than a friend. I guess in ways she *is* a sister to me—a soul sister. The closest I've come to describing her role in my life is with a Celtic word: *anamchara*. It's a word the pagan Celts used to describe a spiritual relationship. After converting to faith in Jesus, the word became layered with the connotations of friendship as a vehicle for spiritual growth. So *anamchara*, loosely translated, means "soul friend."

Cheri and I met almost twenty years ago at Wheaton College. She was into theatre, and I into music. Something about her felt familiar, yet totally foreign to me. Being friends with her was like watching a really good movie with subtitles. From the start, she was someone I wanted to know, someone to whom I wanted to tell every detail of my life. She was the one I told about my hopeless crush on one of the leaders at my church. She was also the one I cried to when he got married.

When we graduated, Cheri married Rich and I married Bryan. And, grace upon saving graces, we wound up living in neighboring Midwestern towns! When both of us got pregnant, Cheri and I served as each other's midwives, and later, as godparents to the respective little ones.

Three years into our idyllic shared *momdom,* Cheri told me that she and her family had to move to Minnesota because of a work opportunity for Rich. I was devastated. Dreams of raising our children together got snuffed out like the candles on a birthday cake. Hopes of summers sitting in lawn chairs and drinking lemonade while our kids played in a fish-shaped plastic pool faded like old family photos. Visions of play dates, walks, annual birthday bashes, and daily talks blurred like my tear-obscured vision. When Cheri moved to Minnesota, I was sure I'd lost my closest friend forever. I never imagined that her move would strengthen our friendship!

During the last three years, I have been shocked with the many unexpected, serendipitous, God-given ways our long-distance friendship has grown. It started with life-preserving, long-distance phone calls. Almost every day, during our children's naps, we'd debrief about our days. Usually I'd cry and complain about my most recent doctor's appointment for lower back pain. She would often share her frustrating journey of trying to make new friends in her community and church. As mothers of toddlers, we felt isolated. Our conversations were life preservers in the stormy sea of motherhood. The phone line was a lifeline to both of us.

Needless to say, after two months and thousands of minutes logged in phone bills, both Cheri and I had to change long-distance carriers. (Happily, we're both on super-saver programs now.)

The frequent, consistent, detail-filled phone calls helped keep our relationship flourishing. But it really began to blossom when we were both bitten by the same bug—the "Writer's Bug." This "bug" is bold, relentless, and quite surreptitious. Its bite caused both of us to start scribbling poems on McDonald's napkins (found underneath our car seats), to wake during the night to write magazine article ideas on the bottoms and sides of shoe boxes in our closets, and to use our church bulletins to transcribe brief book proposals while pretending to take notes on sermons.

Our paths were woven even more tightly when we coauthored a book on friendship and faith titled *Walk with Me* (FaithWalk Publishing, 2005). One section of the book is dedicated to the significance of writing in our lives. In that section, I quote a letter that I wrote to Cheri in May of 2002. Here's part of that letter:

Dear Cheri,

I want you to know again how tickled I am to be sharing the writer's bug with you....

The following string of words is my attempt to express the partnering in so many ways with you: mothering, writing, and just plain daily living.

Talking quilt
Purple days
Endless words
Ribbon maze

Dawn craze
Sleepy haze

I must write
Inspired delight

Discipline provoked
Heaven stoked

Glory be
Little me

Bug catches
Freedom hatches

Friend driven
Gift given[2]

Almost four years after Cheri's move, and because of this ebullient little bug, it feels like Cheri is closer to my heart than ever. She's still the one with whom I want to share all of the details of my life. Even though her home is hundreds of miles from mine, writing and relating has become a home of its own where our friendship resides. Despite the long-distance nature of our relationship, I hook my hands-free "Madonna Phone" over my ear every Tuesday, and we debrief about our weekend. On Fridays she calls me to rehash every detail of her women's Bible study.

If either of us finishes a good book, our phone lines create a cross-country literary link. Our virtual book clubs often last for days. Another link for us is the internet where we send seedling writings back and forth for editing and edification. Even as I write, we're planning a trip to southern Illinois to begin promoting our book—another unexpected link.

My tears shed at Cheri's move were in vain. From my limited perspective, I could only imagine our friendship flourishing if we lived in close proximity to one another. But the reality is that I live in Chicago and she lives in Minneapolis. We're geographically almost 400 miles apart. What a surprise it is to feel *more* connected today than we did when we shared the same dorm room at Wheaton College. Only God could have foreseen the paradox of a close long-distance friend.

When a man leaves home, he leaves behind some scrap of his heart....It's the same with a place a man is going to. Only then he sends a scrap of his heart ahead.[3]

FREDERICK BUECHNER

God Talk—God's Abode

You hem me in—behind and before; you have laid your hand upon me. Such knowledge is too wonderful for me, too lofty for me to attain. Where can I go from your Spirit? Where can I flee from your presence? If I go up to the heavens, you are there; if I make my bed in the depths, you are there....When I awake, I am still with you.

PSALM 139:5-8,18

God's ways are wrought with wildness and the wonder of paradox: a baby born of a virgin; Jesus, a God-man; a wounded Healer; life after death; strength through weakness; and close long-distance friends. Everywhere we look in the Bible there are paradoxes, even when contemplating God's home.

Where is God's home? Sometimes I feel like Job, going everywhere and still having a difficult time finding Him: "But if I go to the east, he is not there; if I go to the west, I do not find him. When he is at work in the north, I do not see him; when he turns to the south, I catch no glimpse of him. But he knows the way that I take" (Job 23:8-10).

The Bible says that "[God] sits enthroned above the circle of the earth....He stretches out the heavens like a canopy, and spreads them out like a tent to live in" (Isaiah 40:22). It also says that He came near to us in Jesus (John 1:14). And God lives in us (John 17:21). For most of my life, I pictured God living in some kind of celestial camp. He seemed far away, and I wondered how my prayers could ever reach *all* the way to the sky where He lived. Then I learned about the paradox of the incarnation and the mystery of Christ in us, the hope of glory (see Colossians 1:27). Living with these irreconcilable truths used to drive me crazy. But I've learned to live with their incomprehensibleness because they help me see the bigness of God.

The belief process is a bit similar to what I went through in realizing that Cheri and I could be close friends even though she lives in Minnesota. My experience with her move and our thriving friendship help me see ways I can be close to God, whose abode is difficult to locate, much less comprehend.

God is a lot like Cheri, my one-state-away, closer-than-a-sister friend. He abides in the heavens, yet is near to me.

He's the one with whom I share my daily, momentary life. I tell Him my hopes and dreams. I share every boring detail of my days with Him because He wants to be close to me. Through Jesus He moved into my neighborhood. And through the Holy Spirit, He lives and moves and breathes in me, a part of His body the church. Just like Cheri, He lives far away, yet in my home and in my heart.

The psalmist proclaims, "Better is one day in your courts than a thousand elsewhere" (Psalm 84:10). When he wrote that, I think he realized that one day we'll be in the heavenly courts of God. At the same time, he must have realized that *any* time we talk to God, we enter His gates. Prayer gives us a connection to God the same way the phone, internet, trips, and books connect me to Cheri.

What a gift to know that we can talk with God in line at the grocery story, in the dark, under the covers, at church, on walks, and in the car. He's *always* near! There's no better place to be than with Him. Our world is His "court" when we choose to be in it with Him. I'm so glad God is accessible—He's here anytime, anywhere.

James solicits us to "come near to God and he will come near to you" (James 4:8). In the same way that I've befriended Cheri and she has befriended me, God is available and present. I get a little giggle knowing that He's right here with me now, even as I write.

His company means even more to me when I'm challenged with the difficult questions that arise when parenting young ones (i.e., discipline, schooling). Or when I'm dealing with a crisis like a car accident, an illness, or a big disappointment. In times like these, it's good to know that He's as available in my daily life as Cheri is. He sees and hears all and offers help and hope.

God is waiting with big shoulders for us to cry on. He lends an ear for our worries. He offers advice when we're confused. And He gives comfort when we feel alone. He welcomes us to His banqueting table. He knows everything about us, and yet He still loves us. And, paradox unequivocal, He's our close long-distance friend.

There is a friend who sticks closer than a brother.

PROVERBS 18:24

Walking the Talk

1. Pray in a place or during a time in which you've never dreamed of praying.

2. Read some biblical passages about heaven. Here are some suggestions: Psalm 8, Psalm 102:25, Isaiah 51:6, and Joel 2:30. Take some time to journal about heaven and where you think God's home is.

3. What are your misconceptions about God's intimacy or distance? List them. Then dispel them with truths about His nearness.

Lord, thank You for being big enough to live in heaven and on Earth. Thanks that I can talk to You anytime, anywhere. Help me be close to You even when You feel faraway. Amen.

Bread vs. Stone; Fish vs. Snake

Prayer as Asking for and Trusting in God's Providence

The best fruits are plucked for each by some hand that is not his own.[1]

C.S. LEWIS

Girl Talk—Billie's Gifts of Grace

Billie Miller is my mother-in-law. Yes, Billie. Her name is indicative of the unique, straightforward yet artistic appeal she possesses. She's not a run-of-the-mill mother-in-law. The best window into her soul is her house.

Billie's home is more like a museum than a residence. It's filled with antiques painted in hues of purple, aqua, and green. Her great room accommodates one of the largest clothespins I've ever seen. Over five feet long, it hangs from a beam by a window overlooking her gardens. The garden's flowers, when in bloom, are as colorful as Billie's personality, her quilts, and her homemade pottery.

Billie's quilts in reds, yellows, blues, and greens are draped over beds and fill armoires. Her pottery, with polka dots, stripes, zigzags and other geometric designs lines kitchen cupboards, and accents bathroom sinks. Navajo rugs, with more graphic designs and vibrant colors, warm her floors. Shaker boxes are stacked next to folk-art chickens and cows, which add to the whimsical country feel of her home.

Whenever I visit Billie's, I feel as if I am visually experiencing the vibrancy and lilt of her spirit. I love looking around Billie's place. Her décor changes with the seasons so there's usually something new and beautiful to see each time.

Billie has the energy of a litter of springer spaniels and the artistic aptitude of Georgia O'Keeffe, Mary Cassatt, and Frida Kahlo rolled into one. Sometimes her energy and perfectionism overwhelm me. Though she never makes me feel that I need to measure up to her standards, I *want* to be like her. I want to have a beautiful, artfully decorated home. But I realize that Bryan and I are on a budget. With two small children, our home will never be fit for the pages of *Better Homes and Gardens*.

Billie not only possesses joie de vivre and an artistic bent, she's also quite gracious, constantly passing gifts on to loved ones who need and will enjoy them. Because Billie has been given abundantly; abundantly she gives. We've received chairs and quilts, goblets and art, jewelry and books, tables and lamps from her. Every time she and her husband, Mike, come to our home for dinner, Mike says, "It's beginning to feel more and more like home here." Clearly that's because more and more of Mike's home is migrating to ours, thanks to Billie!

When Bryan and I got married, we chose not to register for fine china. Instead, we received practical, everyday plates. They're great; we still use them. Months into my marriage, Billie noticed that I enjoy throwing tea parties for my girlfriends. The parties are lovely (even with my everyday dishes) because friends bring flowers to dress up the table and I add napkins in a variety of folds: roses, hats, pockets, and so forth.

Being a gracious gift-giver, Billie invited me over for a tea of her own. Sandwiches of cucumber with cream cheese and dill, tuna and avocado, and green apples with brie lined her table like miniature sculptural pieces of art. As we drank our tea, I felt thankful that my mother-in-law has become one of my dear friends.

At the end of the tea, Billie walked me into the front room where three large boxes were stacked on top of each other. "These are for you," she said. "It's my china. I think you'll use and enjoy it more than I do."

The plates, cups, saucers, and teapot in the set are milk white with a thin silver line tracing each delicate edge. They're beautiful! I use them for all of my teas now. It's funny, but I didn't even realize how much I would enjoy a gift of such dainty beauty until it was given to me. Billie knew my heart's desire even before I did.

She knows me well, watches me, observes my life and my wants and needs. Billie has a knack for knowing the heartbeats of each of her *seven* (yes, seven) children and their spouses. She gives things that delight and gifts that rescue. Her gifts have often been our salvation when we've been in the middle of some of life's pickles.

When we were engaged to be married, for example, Bryan had a horrible accident with his Skill saw. He was creating some intricate trim for a customer's ceiling when he noticed a splattering of blood on the wall. It was *his* blood. When Bryan looked down at his hand, he realized that the top part of his middle finger was hanging on by a mere strip of skin.

He was rushed to the emergency room, and his digit was repaired. But the hospital bills were extensive, even with insurance. Billie knew we were just starting out, and she paid all of the uncovered expenses. What a gracious gift!

When I think about all of the gifts Billie has given me, I realize that she gave the most precious one before she even met me. This gift was her decision to conceive and carry a *seventh* child, a son—Bryan, my husband.

God Talk—God as Giver of Good Things

*Your Father knows what you need
before you ask him.*

MATTHEW 6:8

Like Billie, God knows His children and gives them good things. When we ask God for something, He answers. Sometimes He rescues us with His gracious gifts. Other times He gives gifts just to bring us delight. God gives us gifts, such as grace, even when it's not our birthday. His presents are not always the ones we expect. But they're gifts nonetheless. And there's a beauty that comes in our asking. It's part of the process of being in a relationship with the God who listens and cares.

Sometimes when we ask God for something, He is slow to answer, so we assume that He's saying no, or He's out of resources. But, like Billie, He has in abundance and He freely gives. The psalms describe God as the owner of "the cattle on a thousand hills" (Psalm 50:10).

God made *everything*. He owns *everything*. The earth is His; its resources are His. The apples, hills, water, oil, grass, grain, watermelons, grapes, cows, and goats—all His. *We* are even His, created for His pleasure: "For you created everything, and it is for your pleasure that they exist and were created" (Revelation 4:11 NLT).

I believe this. I perceive God as owner, architect, landscaper, and purveyor of the universe. Yet I sometimes doubt. When for years I wanted a husband, I doubted God's providence. When I wanted a daughter but could not carry another child due to chronic back pain, I doubted. When I see commercials about starving children in Ethiopia, I doubt. When I read stories about overflowing orphanages in China, Russia, and Guatemala—again I doubt.

If God has the resources, why are His children starving, homeless, or motherless? Why is the world full of disease, poverty, and war? Why doesn't He seem to be answering our prayers? I don't have the answers. But I believe God is good (Psalm 34:8). And that He will ultimately provide for *all* of us with heavenly grace. I choose to believe His promise, "I will not leave you as orphans; I will come to you" (John 14:18). "I have loved you with an everlasting love; I have drawn you with loving-kindness. I will build you up again" (Jeremiah 31:3-4). I also believe that while we're living in a cruel world where famine, disease, and death are part of the deal, God uses *us* as His hands and feet in a needy world. "Pure and lasting religion in the sight of God our Father means that we must care for orphans and widows in their troubles" (James 1:27 NLT).

Sometimes I wonder what would happen if Americans stopped paying thousands of dollars for tickets to NBA basketball games, hundreds of bucks for designer shoes, and loads of loot on fast, foreign cars. Maybe if we could curb some of our excessive indulgences and give more freely, the world would start to change. I know many wealthy and not-so-wealthy folks are philanthropic. But what if we *all* were? I wonder what would happen if *I* started sacrificing a little bit more in order to help others who are in need.

I'm not suggesting that God does not want us to enjoy our lives. He does. "I came that they may have life, and have it abundantly," God says in John 10:10 NASB. He gives sunsets, hand-me-down quilts and china, paintings and poetry, sports and leisure just for us. God *wants* us to enjoy our lives fully...abundantly. At the same time, I think He's calling us, calling me, to follow His lead and Billie's example to give more generously to others.

Maybe it'll make our giving more joyful if we believe God's promise that "even strong young lions sometimes go hungry, but those who trust in the LORD will never lack any good thing" (Psalm 34:10 NLT). And maybe we'll see that the actual ability to trust God for our needs is another one of His gifts.

If we see God as protective and providential as a mother lion fiercely hunting food for her cubs, maybe we'll get a picture of His true regard for our needs. God *is* on the hunt. Often He moves in the world in ways we can't see or understand. Still, He is on the move. He provided a husband for me, later in my life, when I least expected it. He gave my husband and me the gift of two sons. And currently, through the gift of adoption, He's giving us a daughter and an orphan a home. To top it all off, He gives us mercy and grace enough for each day.

Jesus asks us, "Which of you, if his son asks for bread, will give him a stone? Or if he asks for a fish, will give him a snake? If you, then, though you are evil, know how to give good gifts to your children, how much more will your Father in heaven give good gifts to those who ask him" (Matthew 7:9-11)! God is good. He loves us. He is more than capable and wants to give us good gifts. All we have to do is trust and ask.

As we come to God in prayer, we can relax in the knowledge that He's a giver of gifts. If we pray for a fish, He'll not send us a scaly, hissing reptile. If we're hungry for a piece of crusty bread, He'll not hand us a big ol' dusty rock. He wants what's best for us and is dying to give us gracious gifts.

Ask and it will be given to you.

MATTHEW 7:7

Walking the Talk

But, God cannot give until a man asks. It is not that He wants to withhold something from us, but that is the plan He has established for the way of redemption. Through our asking God puts His process in motion, creating something in us that was nonexistent until we asked.[2]

OSWALD CHAMBERS

1. How has God provided for you? Make a list of His good and perfect gifts. Thank Him!

2. Think of some ways you can pass His gracious gifts on to others. Do it.

3. Have you ever considered that God's good, perfect, and abundant gifts are His ways of declaring His love for you? You may want to think or write about this.

Charity—giving to the poor—is an essential part of Christian morality.…I do not believe one can settle how much we ought to give. I am afraid the only safe rule is to give more than we can spare. In other words, if our expenditure on comforts, luxuries, amusements, etc., is up to the standard common among those with the same income as our own, we are probably giving away too little.[3]

C.S. LEWIS

Father, I know that You own the cattle of all the hills and that You are a generous benefactor. Thank You for giving to me abundantly and in ways that clearly communicate Your love for me. May I follow in kind—giving generously to others as a token of my love for You. Amen.

5

This Song's for You

Belting Out Prayers

Shout for joy to the LORD, all the earth.
Worship the LORD with gladness;
come before him with joyful songs.

PSALM 100:1

Girl Talk—Pam and the Letter that Taught Me to Sing

When I was in eighth grade, Pam—a.k.a. Miss Mays—was my music teacher. When she sang, her warm alto seemed to hug me. When she taught, her enthusiasm and knowledge took me on musical safaris. And when she talked about God, her authenticity and grace swirled around me like a sonata. Pam taught me about the color, form, texture, rhythm, and style of music. She also taught me to sing my prayers.

Looking back to junior high days, I remember a time in study hall when Pam was the monitor. It was a snowy day. I sat in the third seat of the first row working on Spanish. Halfway through the period, I heard Pam's heels clicking on the linoleum floor. She neared my desk. When I looked up, Miss Mays handed me a powder-blue envelope.

"Open it whenever you want," she said, and then she walked back to her desk at the front of the room and sat down.

I turned the envelope over and over in my hand. *Should I wait to open it? No.* I tore into it, and read the following:

Dear Sally,

I guess you're wondering why I'm writing you instead of just talking to you. So...I'll "drop the bomb" as they say, right away. I've been thinking and praying about this for quite a while.

I was wondering if you and Julie (and any others who would be open to this) would be interested in meeting one or two times each week for a prayertime or Bible study or to sing Christian songs (sort of a praise time)—OR we could do all three!

Since we'd be meeting on school property, we'll have to clear this with the principal. Also, if the idea sounds good, please clear it with your parents, too.

Please do much thinking and praying about this, and share my letter with people you feel would be interested. Nothing excites me more than the thought of sharing with you the love of our Lord in song, prayer, and Bible study.

Love, Miss Mays

I didn't have to think or pray. My heart was racing as fast as a hummingbird's. I looked up at Miss Mays, smiled broadly, and gave her the thumbs up.

For almost two years following that letter, Pam, some of my friends, and I met on Thursdays at the crack of dawn. The best part of our meeting was when we sang our hearts out to God: "Love Him in the morning when you see the sun arising"…"I cast all my cares upon You; I lay all of my burdens down at Your feet"…"No other love, no other love, no other love is like Your love."

Our voices were never quite warmed up. In fact, I can remember Pam using the capo on her guitar, frequently lowering the keys of our songs. I'm sure we sounded more like a bullfrog chorus than an angelic choir. But I don't think God minded. And we didn't either. We were glad to be alive, together, and singing our prayers.

About a decade after our morning croak sessions, I graduated from Wheaton College with a bachelor's in Music Education. Following in Pam's footsteps, I became a music teacher. And, serendipitously, I got a job teaching in the *same* district where Pam works!

As we taught together for ten years, Pam mentored me in the tools of the trade. At the same time, she became one of my dearest friends. During that season of my life, I was unhappily single. So Pam graciously walked with me through a bevy of boyfriends. We met at Boloney's during many lunch hours. I'd cry in my soup. She'd listen and pray. When I finally met and married Bryan, she stood beside me at the wedding. Before the service, I gathered with a group of girlfriends and sang the songs Pam had taught me.

Those songs, sung for the first time in the corner room at my junior high, have found their way into the crevices of my soul. Even now their melodies and lyrics surface at pivotal moments in my days. They help reconnect me to God.

Just as Pam has become a lifelong friend, living with me through the changing seasons, so have her songs. Time and again, they take me by the hand and heart and bring me back to God.

Let the word of Christ dwell in you richly as you teach and admonish one another with all wisdom, and as you sing psalms, hymns and spiritual songs with gratitude in your hearts to God.

COLOSSIANS 3:16

God Talk—The Giver and Maker of Music

He put a new song in my mouth, a hymn of praise.

PSALM 40:3

Because of Pam, I realized that music is one of God's greatest gifts. When I'm fumbling for words in my prayers, God inevitably gives me the gift of a song to help me to His throne of grace. Lyrics, or even just a tune, often help me connect with Him in conversation and praise.

God has been in the business of giving the gift of song to His people for ages. He gave songs to King David over and over again. (In fact, the book of Psalms is actually an ancient hymnal, written primarily by the king.) The Bible is packed with examples of God's people receiving the gift of song.

Long after biblical times, God continues to extend the gift of music. He gave music to me, through Pam. He gives it to Amy Grant, Bruce Cockburn, Barry Manilow, church music ministers, rock-n-rollers, James Taylor, U2, Third Day, and many other music makers. God graciously gives music as a tool that enables us to speak more freely to Him than mere words allow.

Picture this. It's October of 1705. A young Johann Sebastian Bach, let's call him Johnny, is walking from Arnstadt to Lübeck, Germany. Johnny is the well-known organist at a huge church in Arnstadt. He really burns up those keys. Johnny's the modern-day equivalent of a rock star like Sting.

Johnny "Sting" Bach tells his church family that he needs to go to Lübeck to meet with another renowned rock star, Buxtehude, whom we'll call Billy Joel. Johnny claims that Billy Joel will show him some riffs that'll send the home congregation into a mosh pit frenzy. The "powers that be" allow Johnny to take the 200-mile trip by foot. Little do they know that their 20-year-old rock star is really going on a jaunt through northern Germany in search of a girlfriend!

Needless to say, on the long dusty journey Johnny has a lot of time to talk to God. And God responds with the gift of music. On that trip the famous *Fugue in G minor* is given, as well as some of Johnny's first cantatas, the modern-day equivalent of top-40 smashes.

The music came to Bach as if wrapped in tissue and tied in a satin bow. J.S. recognized the Giver. So he wrote S.D.G. *(Soli Deo Gloria),* only God gets the glory, on each of the pieces. Then he taught them to the musicians at his church. These musicians sang Bach's works at church, effectively returning God's gift in an offering of praise.

God gave the gift of music to Bach. Bach gave it to the people. Then the people gave it back to God. God to Bach...and Bach again: a full circle of musical gift giving.

I wonder if Pam felt the way Bach did? God gave her songs. She shared them with me. Together we returned the gift to Him. And we still do.

Music is God's gift to man, the only art of heaven given to earth, And the only art of earth we take to heaven.[1]

WALTER SAVAGE LANDER

Walking the Talk

To sing is to pray twice.

ANONYMOUS

1. Dust off your old hymnal or collection of praise songs. Gather a group of your girlfriends and sing until your hearts are content.

2. Write a personal psalm, hymn, or praise song. Sing it to God at the top of your lungs. (Strive for authenticity over perfection.)

3. Listen to a symphony or another of your favorite CDs. Try to hear what God is saying to you through the music.

Maker of Music, thanks for the gift of song and people with whom I can sing. Please accept my prayers, requests, and praises that waft in melodic, harmonious tune or just as joyous noise. Amen.

A Woman of Words

Written Prayers

*I've been playing with words...in the
pages of my journal since I was fourteen.
Often it seems I just catch my heart and
mind's dictation and take notes.*[1]

SUSAN GOLDSMITH WOOLDRIDGE

Girl Talk—Cheri's Journal

Even before Cheri started freelance writing, she was always a writer at heart. We shared a house with five other women during our senior year at Wheaton College. She had a bungalow room comprised mainly of windows that butted up to a large oak tree. Sitting in her room was like sitting in a tree house. It was there that Cheri often wrote.

I have vivid memories of Cheri sitting in her tree-house perch working on a journal with music from the *"Say Anything"* soundtrack blasting in the background. Her journal was a ragtag collage of words and ideas housed in a spiral notebook. She filled it with poems, essays, and other random thoughts. She also included photos, scraps of fabric, magazine clippings, sketches, and quotes from her favorite books. I had a burning desire to snoop through her journal. I felt about the journal the same way I feel about Cheri—like it's a treasure waiting to be discovered.

The only time I ever got to read any of Cheri's journals was one day in December of 1989. I was begging to see some of the sketches and so forth in her new journal. Smiling, she handed it to me opened to a page where the following quotation was scrawled: "[A] prayer journal is not something for anyone else's eyes, and so the matter of guarding the privacy of one's journal must be considered before beginning it. Any 'open' prayer journal is unlikely to be a *real* one. Even the fear that someone will invade the privacy of its pages can keep a soul from the searching kind of honesty that should go into it. —Leanne Payne"[2]

That was that. From then on, the only times I ever caught sight of Cheri's journal was when she was working on it. The rest of the time it was hidden. And when Cheri finished a journal, she religiously burned it. Up in smoke went hours of ideas, imaginations, and insights that she'd shared with God. Maybe the fire and fumes were prayer offerings in themselves. Nevertheless, it pained me to see the surreptitious scrapbooks of sorts go up in smoke.

Before I met Cheri, my journals were the store bought variety. At first I used black or burgundy with gold leaf pages and crosses on the covers. Then I graduated in grace to some of the more feminine varieties covered in floral cloth. My journals simply contained some of my general feelings about life and my prayer requests and God's answers.

Cheri agreed that that was *one* way of keeping a prayer journal. But she thought our written prayers could change and develop as radically as the seasons. "There's no way our words with God should be constrained by formats or formulas," she said. "When my heart is living in a cold, dark season like winter, sometimes all I can write and pray is

"Help, Lord!" Other times, when it feels as if it's springtime in my heart, everything is budding and bursting forth, my journal is filled with sonnets, supplications, and songs. In seasons of summer, when I'm feeling playful and light, I find myself writing dramas and poetry that become my prayers."

This enlarged way of praying bothered me. It seemed almost irreverent and definitely unorthodox. First of all, I couldn't imagine writing a play. And second, I wondered how a *poem* could possibly be a prayer. But Cheri's creativity with words inspired me to try new things in my journals, to become more playful, experimental, joyful, creative, and childlike.

Recently when I went to visit Cheri and her family in Minnesota, I wasn't surprised to see that Jennifer, Cheri's five-year-old daughter, had a Hello Kitty journal. She sat on her bed and wrote in it as she sang the following home-grown poem:

> I love the world singing bye;
> the crows come and eat the seeds in the summer.
> I love the winter singing bye, when the leaves go
> to sleep.
> I love everyone of God. I tell Him truth. Sometimes
> I get mad.

Jen has already learned what I didn't discover until my collegiate days: Words can be rhythmic, imaginative, playful, born out of the seasons of life. Her writings are lovely and sincere. I don't know exactly what they all mean, but they speak of life and death, singing and telling the truth to God. Her mother's influence has been cellular and profound.

Jen journals anytime, anywhere. Sometimes she writes at the kitchen table while she eats breakfast. Other days she jots journal entries in an overstuffed chair in the family room while her brothers play on the carpet. Jen's siblings clearly communicate with God, too. Journaling's just not for them. It's not for everyone. We all have unique ways of communicating with our Creator. For souls like Cheri and Jen, journaling is an oblation instead of an obligation. Like juice from an orange, words just pour out of them.

All poetry is prayer.

SAMUEL BECKETT

God Talk—God as Writer

I will put my laws in their minds and
write them on their hearts. I will be their God,
and they will be my people.

HEBREWS 8:10

When I think of God as a writer, two images emerge. One is of a being in a celestial sort of London. He's bald, dressed in a tweed jacket, and smoking a pipe. Glasses crown his nose. He's a C.S. Lewis look-alike sitting behind a simple desk of cherry, typing on a manual typewriter. A nearby garbage can overflows, creating a crumpled carpet of paper at his feet.

My other image of God as writer takes me to ancient Egypt. Here I see God as the *queset ha-sopher*, a scribe who appeared to Ezekiel. He's clothed in white linen and is carrying a writing case brimming with papyrus, pens, styluses, brushes, vials of colored ink, and an ink stone. The tips of his fingers are stained black from writing; his brow is brown and sweaty. He hurries down a dusty path looking for a shady place to sit and scribe.

Neither of these is a very accurate nor documented description. However, as they give insights into different types of writers, they help us imagine God writing. A passage in 2 Corinthians helps, too. Here, Paul gives his friends in Corinth a poignant description of God as writer:

> You yourselves are our letter, written on our hearts, known and read by everybody. You show that you are a letter from Christ, the result of our ministry, written not with ink but with the Spirit of the living God, not on tablets of stone but on tablets of human hearts (2 Corinthians 3:2-3).

God's writing is unlike any writing Cheri, Jen, you, or I will ever do. His letters (or journal entries, if you will) are people. People who walk around and tell His story...people who speak His words, live His truths, honor His message. He uses His Spirit to write His love notes on the very tablets of our hearts.

The first time we read about God writing on tablets is in Exodus. Here we see Him as He asks Moses to come up to the holy mountain and receive tablets of stone with written commands (Exodus 24:12): the Ten Commandments. Forty days later, Moses returns with two tablets inscribed on both sides, and "the writing was the writing of God, engraved on the tablets" (Exodus 32:16).

Wow! What I would have given to see God's actual writing! I wonder what it looked like. Was it curly cursive or in block letters? Was it deeply engraved or was it more wispy and scrolly? The way someone writes tells so much about him or her. It would've been fun to see those supernatural scribbles. I guess in some ways, when we look at one another, we get the best glimpses of God's handwriting we'll ever see.

If God took the time to write the Ten Commandments in His own hand, He must care about written words. Maybe He even keeps a journal like Cheri's! Regardless, the word "word" shows up more than 500 times in the Bible. God uses words to communicate with us. He tells us about the world around us and about Himself through writings on our hearts.

Because God values words, so should His people. As long as 5,000 years ago, in ancient China, people verily valued the written word and used it to express themselves. Calligraphy (the writing of Chinese characters) was more than just a way to communicate. It was an art form believed to actually embody the words it represented. The very characters transcended their symbolic scratches and squiggles. To the Chinese, characters were almost spiritual, living. It was believed that words brushed, engraved, or carved actually possessed power to move and effect changes in the world.[3]

A similar phenomenon occurred much later, in first-century Palestine. There, a Jewish sect called the Pharisees valued the written word just as much as the Chinese. The Pharisees actually wore frontlets, or *phylacteries* (Matthew 23:5), which were small leather boxes containing parchment laden with the words and laws of God. These phylacteries were strapped to the forehead with leather thongs or they were worn on the arm so that "when a person crossed his arms the Scriptures [or words of God] contained in the phylactery would be close to the heart."[4]

Unfortunately, some Pharisees wore excessively large frontlets. God's words were abused in a kind of spiritual snobbery. It reminds me of the way modern folks paste poor paraphrases of God's Word on bumper stickers. However, pious proselytizing like this should not discourage us from holding God's precious words close to our hearts.

Words are powerful. They move us. They find a way into the depths of our beings. They can be used to bless or curse, name or blaspheme. Just think of the wide range of ways we use our words: writing poems, whispering affectionate words to a loved one, sharing silly giggles and knock-knock jokes with girlfriends, or yelling at people who cut us off in traffic.

King David was a wordsmith. His psalms, literally "songs," were penned in much the same way as Cheri and Jen's journals. They were simple outpourings of his heart through the ups and downs in his life. They were his way of asking God, 'Search me...and know my heart; test me and know my anxious thoughts" (Psalm 139:23). They were filled with blessings, questions, anger, and love for God.

Sharing our honest thoughts with God through written or spoken words is one of the first steps in our prayer journey. Being honest means following King David's lead. "We must lay before Him what is in us, not what ought to be in us."[5] Prayer is about sharing our anger, sadness, fears, and disappointments, as well as our joys and praises. If we're open with ourselves and God, then we'll be able to more clearly hear His words for us. And while we reveal our hearts to God, He will actually write His words on our hearts.

Walking the Talk

For me the disciplines of writing and praying are ever closer and closer together, each a letting go of our own will and an opening up to the power of God's will.[6]

MADELEINE L'ENGLE

1. What is your relationship with words? Do you like them, or do they intimidate you? Why?

2. If you consider yourself a "writer type," start (or continue) a prayer journal.

3. If you have old journals, take some time to read them.

4. Make some tea and enjoy a poetry collection alone or with a girlfriend. What is God saying to you in the words? If you're feeling inspired, write your own poem prayer.

5. If you could see the words God has written on your heart today, what do you think the lettering would look like? Is it deeply etched, slightly scratched, curly, block...? What do you think the words say? Why?

Author and Perfector, thank You for writing on blocks of stone and on my heart. Help me recognize Your written words and even write a few in return. Amen.

It's O.K. to Play

Laughter and Prayer

There is a time for everything…
a time to weep and a time to laugh.

ECCLESIASTES 3:1,4

Girl Talk—Hannah's Sense of Humor

Hannah is one of the funniest women I know. She has an uncanny ability to find humor in ordinary life. Whenever I need a good laugh, she's the one I call. She brings lightness to my days with her witty winsomeness and prankster personality. She truly understands that laughter is the best medicine (Proverbs 17:22).

Every year I host an ornament-making party during Advent. My closest friends gather by the fire, string cranberries, and drink wassail. Hannah inevitably brings a gag hostess gift. Last year she handed me a box. Inscribed on the card was this rhyme:

You've been naughty that's the scoop.
All you get is snowman poop.

I lifted the lid to find five puffy, jumbo-sized marshmallows nestled inside.

Hannah has a way of making almost any moment lighthearted. I was with her when she gave birth to her first child. It was a long labor. After more than forty hours, Hannah finally dilated to ten centimeters. It was time for her to push. Everyone in the room, including her husband and midwife, was exhausted and fearful. We were worried that after the treacherous, back-stabbing labor, she wouldn't have the strength to get the baby through the birth canal.

After three pushes, and in the throes of another contraction, Hannah cried out, "Can I get a stunt double in here...PLEEEEASE?" Everyone in the room doubled over in laughter. Hannah bore down, and Max was born.

A comedian at heart, Hannah's gift of humor helps her cope in life. It also brings lots of smiles my way. Time after time, when I'm laboring with a problem, Hannah helps me see the lighter side. One day, I was talking to my friend on the phone. I told her that I was concerned about not feeding my kids three square meals a day and about our frequent stops at McDonalds. She giggled and said, "I guess I'm *really* in trouble with the Nutrition Squad then. Last night, as a practical joke, I gave my kids 'mashed potatoes and gravy' that was really ice cream doused in caramel sauce." Hannah and I giggled and found refreshment in the shared burden of cooking for a full house.

Hannah always gives me the freedom to laugh at myself and all the absurdity found in life. She follows in Sarah's steps. In Genesis, Sarah, a woman barren for years, learns to celebrate and laugh at life's absurd twists. In her old age, she gives birth to a son. When he's born, she names him Isaac, which means "laughter." Holding Isaac, Sarah declares, "God has brought me laughter, and everyone who hears about this will laugh with me" (Genesis 21:6).

Like Sarah, Hannah laughs at the improbable punch lines of the Lord. And she invites others to chuckle along with her. I'm happy to say that my laughter quotient has doubled since I met Hannah. And my heart is glad to see the humorous side of God through her.

A good laugh is as good as a prayer sometimes.[1]
LUCY MAUD MONTGOMERY

God Talk—A Lover of Laughter

God made the music of laughter and gave us our smiles. He's not too holy to handle throw-your-head-back laughter. He's the one who created it! Unfortunately, most pictures portray Jesus as solemn and sad. This really bugged Hannah, so she jumped for joy when Ralph Kozak painted a portrait called "Jesus Laughing." She carries a wallet-sized copy in her purse.

Jesus must have done a lot of laughing. He spent most of His adult life with a troupe of gangly guy friends who walked together, slept together, and ate every meal together. I can picture Him punching his buddies' arms with playful, inside jokes about Peter's overzealous nature and John's soft side. I can hear Jesus whooping and hollering with the gang as they tell tall fishing tales.

When I read the Bible with God's sense of humor in mind, jokes appear at every turn. Just the other day I was reading in the book of Numbers. I encountered a story about the Israelites in the middle of their 40-year jaunt through the desert. They were sick and tired of eating manna, so they complained to Moses, "If only we had meat to eat! We remember the fish we ate in Egypt at no cost—also the cucumbers, melons, leeks, onions and garlic. But now we have lost our appetite; we never see anything but this manna!" (Numbers 11:4-6).

The next day God sent down showers of quails. In fact, He gave them so much meat that it began to come out of their nostrils and they began to loathe it (Numbers 11:20). I can just see God cracking up on His heavenly throne. Instead of warning the Israelites about their complaining, He gave them what they asked for...and it was funny.

I think God loves to laugh. He endorses laughter and cheer over and over:

- filling Job's mouth with laughter (Job 8:21)

- loving cheerful givers (2 Corinthians 9:7)

- recommending laughter as good medicine (Proverbs 17:22)

- encouraging us to take heart or be of good cheer (John 16:33)

Unfortunately, when I think of communing with God, laughter is not the first thing that comes to mind. Instead I usually picture a more solemn kind of connection. Solemnity *is* part of my prayer life. But Hannah has helped me realize that conversations with God should not exclude a human, humorous, lighthearted kind of connection. Though I can cry to God and sit with Him in silence, it is also O.K. to laugh, hoot, and smile during my talks with Him.

One evening Hannah and I were praying together. I had been struggling with some chronic back pain. She came over to pray for help and healing. Our dinner must've been exceptionally rich that night because I was extremely flatulent during her prayers. The first time I "fluffed," Hannah kept right on praying. But the third "toot" sounded as resonant as a high A on a French horn.

Mid prayer, Hannah combusted into a fit of laughter. It came out of her mouth in hoots and from her nose in snorts! Her fit was contagious, and I began laughing, too. The room roared with our ruckus. I think God must've been having a chuckle right along with us. In fact, the laughter we shared became our prayer.

Walking the Talk

Healthy prayer necessitates frequent experiences of the common, earthy, run-of-the-mill variety. Like walks, and talks, and good wholesome laughter...[2]

RICHARD J. FOSTER

1. Check out a book of jokes from the library. Tell a few to a friend. Share a laugh.

2. Tell a joke to God. Listen for His laughter. Then look for one of His jokes in your life, in His Word, and in the world.

3. The next time you're praying with a friend, don't be afraid to laugh. It's O.K.

4. Celebrate laughter in your life by renting a funny movie or CD. Enjoy it with a friend. Realize that God loves it when His daughters giggle.

5. Thank God for the gift of laughter.

Lord, thank You for jokes shared among friends. Thanks also for Your own joyful, funny side. Help me laugh more often with You. Amen.

8

Telling It Like It Is

Prayers of Confession

*Confess your sins to each other
and pray for each other so that
you may be healed.*

JAMES 5:16

Girl Talk—Cheri and the Diary of a Mad White Woman

It had been a capital 'B' Bad day. Normally I'm in bed by
nine o'clock. But this night the clock was ticking toward ten
thirty, and I was still up scribbling in my diary like a mad
woman. I had already scrawled red ink across five pages.
And I knew that I had five left in me. But I began to cry ugly
and couldn't scribble another word.

My husband heard me. "What's wrong, Babe?" he asked.

"I've failed as a mother. I'm the worst mom on the planet.
The Cat in the Hat would be a better mom than I am."

Bryan could see I was hysterical. For ten minutes he tried
to "fix me." He got out the proverbial toolbox and went to
work. He told me to get some sleep because everything
would look brighter in the morning. He even came up with
a plan of attack for my next day of mothering.

That made me cry harder! My shoulders were slumped. My spirit was deflated. My face looked like a leaky red potato.

Gently and helplessly Bryan said, "Sal, I know it's late. But why don't you try calling Cheri. I have a feeling she'll know just what you need."

Bryan was right. When I'm overwhelmed with sins and shortcomings relating to mothering or anything else, talking to Cheri usually helps. She *gets* the struggles of early motherhood. Like me, she's in the trenches of toddler years—in the thick of it, so to speak—so she's equipped with the healing balm of compassionate grace and gentleness when I need it most.

I dialed her number. The phone rang three times. I was worried about waking her, but she sounded lively when she answered, almost singing her greeting: "Hello."

"Cheri? Can you talk?" I asked.

"Sure, I'm up nursing the baby. He's having a tough time going to sl..."

Before she could finish, a down-pouring of tears and a deluge of declarations descended. "It's been a bad day, Cher," I said. "Before breakfast, I dropped a gallon of Oberweiss milk. It shattered on the kitchen floor like a hand grenade...I swore in front of the kids....then apologized while I swept up the mess...I must've missed one piece 'cause it pierced Ben's foot and he had to get three stitches....In a mad rush to preschool, I forgot to bring Ayden's show-and-tell...I have a column due next week... so instead of taking the boys outside to play this afternoon, I let them watch three videos...I forgot to defrost our lasagna for dinner...cooked it anyway...when I served it, the top was burned and the center was still icy cold.

"I'm the *worst* mother on the planet. I've wounded and abandoned my kids. My writing's rushed. My dinners are disgusting, and…

Before I could finish the next self-deprecating sentence, Cheri said, "Sal, you're one of the best moms I know. I think you've just had one of those days. We all have them. Our plates are too full, our patience is thin, and our kids are antsy for attention. If it makes you feel any better, when Rich got home tonight, he asked what I did all day. I pointed to the bathroom and said, 'I cleaned half a toilet…and the brush is still in it as proof.'"

We both laughed out loud. Then she asked, "May I pray for you?"

"Yes," I said, with moisture in my eyes and a turned around frown.

Her prayer felt as warm as an embrace. When she finished, though my eyes were swollen and my nose clogged, I felt a little lighter.

As Cheri and I share the burden and blessing of motherhood, we inescapably obey one biblical instruction. It's found in the epistle of James: "Confess your sins to each other and pray for each other so that you may be healed" (James 5:16). Confessing sins and shortcomings to Cheri is easy. She knows me. She doesn't judge me. Instead, she offers gentle grace and assurance. And to help me feel comfortable, she freely shares her own humanness. I'm so thankful that she understands.

God Talk—The Gentle Human Healer

*Jesus' total embrace of humanity, His becoming like us,
is the basis of our hope to someday be like Him.*[1]

MICHAEL CARD

When we confess, God meets us in the moment with gentleness. He sees and understands our humanness. Instead of condemning us for our sins and shortcomings, He understands and offers grace just like my friend Cheri did.

As I mentioned, Cheri "gets me" and my faults because she's a mom. God "gets me" and my frailty because He was human. It's hard to believe, isn't it? But Hebrews 5:2 NLT says, "[Every high priest] is human, he is able to deal gently with the people...for he is subject to the same weaknesses they have." Jesus is our high priest.

I know it feels almost theologically incorrect or just plain uncomfortable having a Savior who was subject to weaknesses. But He was. And, as sad as that makes me for Jesus, it also makes me glad—glad to know that He really understands the human plight.

I'm thankful that God did not choose to remain a lofty, in the clouds, kind of God. I'm thankful that He became a wholly human God. He got blisters from His sandals. He had body odor when it was hot and humid. He got tired at the ends of long days. His stomach hurt if He ate food that was too rich.

Though He was infallible, He still knew the sting of heartbreak and humanity. He cried. He was denied by a best friend. He dropped His cross on the way to Calvary. His muscles got sore. He had bruises. He saw pain in His mother's eyes. He was pierced with a spear. He died.

God fully understands what it feels like to live within the broken confines of humanness. God "gets us" just like Cheri "gets" me. Because of this, our confessions can come out of a place of shared suffering not shame. He sees us. He knows us. He "gets" how hard it is to be human. Because of this, He *deals gently* with us.

The other day, a spiritual bigwig of sorts, who shall remain nameless, visited my women's Bible study. At the end of our group meeting, he asked in a rather piously condescending tone, "Do you confess your sins one to another?"

At first, I felt a wave of guilt crash over me. *No. We don't...and we must be falling short of the church's expectations of our meetings*, I thought. Then, after he left, I thought more about his question. *Yes, we confess our sins to each other*, I wish I would've said. *Of course we confess our sins to one another! We do it every day on the phone, at the grocery store, the mall, or over e-mail!*

And when we don't have time to share with our friends, our children constantly clarify our confessions for us. Like little foghorns blaring our faults, they declare our blunders, blemishes, and imperfections everywhere. At McDonalds, the pool, the park: "Mommy, you never play with me the way Tyler's mommy does" or "I liked your long hairdo better" or "You hurt my feelings when you yelled at me, Mama."

Of course women confess sins to one another! Inevitably, in the course of our daily conversations, the confessions of "mad" mothers just come up. We *need* to speak our hearts. We easily and freely declare and acknowledge our shortcomings—they're unavoidable.

Confessing sins does not have to be a lofty, formal, or pious practice. It can be as simple as sharing the events of a bad day over the phone with a friend. Most of the time confessing a sin right in the moment, in front of our crying children, an exasperated boss, or a harried husband is the best thing we can do. This is not to say that weekend retreats for contemplation and confession are not valuable. Or that early-morning moments or late-night times of confession are not worth the effort. All I'm pointing out is that organic, daily confessions between friends and God are just as *real* as mornings spent meditating on which of the Ten Commandments we've broken.

No matter what the means of our confessions, the good news is God's grace. When we acknowledge that there's mud, muck, and dead grass in the yards of our lives, He provides a blanket of freshly fallen snow: *Grace*. A fresh start.

For me, these fresh starts come when I'm honest on the phone with Cheri. They come in the moments of my days when I'm honest with God about my inadequacies. *Lord, I'm sorry that I've been thinking more about my book than I've been thinking about You. Help me see You in the process. Father, forgive me for losing my temper with the boys. Please give me a drop of Your patience. I'm sorry for my selfishness in my marriage. Help me to find space to serve Bryan.*

Any time I confess my sins in prayer, something funny happens. My faith seems to flower. God takes my seed of honest confession and grows it into a confession of faith. My prayers become less and less about my faults and more and more about God's work in my life. Speaking truthfully about impatience is the sprout that grows into a plant of patience. Sharing openly about selfishness is the shoot that yields a vine of service. A confession of jealousy often brings about the fruit of joy for the successes of others.

The process of confession reminds me that God takes our confusion, imperfections, brokenness, and strife and makes something beautiful out of the prayer of our lives.

Walking the Talk

We follow a Savior who conquers by allowing Himself to be conquered, who saves us by not allowing Himself to be saved. He bids us follow in the same way. The fact of His humanity is our hope for salvation.[2]

MICHAEL CARD

1. If you've had a bad day, call a friend and share your struggles. Ask her to pray for you.

2. As a way of confessing sin, make a list that shares some of your human frailties with God. For example: selfishness, pride, dishonesty, jealousy, distrust. Then ask God to reveal a new list of faith-filled words to confess, such as service, humility, honesty, love, trust.

3. Think of some ways God has reached beyond justice to grace in your life. Thank Him!

Forgiving Father, I am truly sorry for hurting You and others. Thank You for hearing my hurtfulness, seeing my shortcomings, and giving me grace. Amen.

9

All Ears

Prayers that Are Heard

> *This communicating of a man's self to [his] friend works two contrary effects, for it redoubleth joy, and cutteth griefs in half.*
>
> FRANCIS BACON

Girl Talk—Jo's Inviting Eyes

Jo is a worship leader at a megachurch that I attended sporadically from junior high until I got married. She's a local celebrity of sorts, though she'd never admit it. With long blond locks and blue saucer eyes, her physical beauty enhances her inner loveliness as she helps lead the sprawling congregation in worship.

I've often wondered why Jo befriended me. Without hesitation she took me under her wing, connected me with other musicians at the church, and ultimately forged a way for me to co-lead a worship team for the church's singles ministry. More importantly, for years she encouraged me to sink my scrawny sapling roots into rich spiritual soil. Strangely enough, Jo did this mostly by listening to me, by attending to my thoughts, concerns, joys, worries, and woes.

There's something special about Jo. When she looks at me, I feel as if I'm the only person on the planet. At church, if she smiles in my general direction during a worship chorus, it feels as if the 4,000-person congregation disappears and it's just God, Jo, and me reveling in a musical torrent.

The sincere, intense brightness in her eyes is warmly inviting. Her attentive spirit and engaging look have a way of getting me to talk. When we go for coffee after church, she's fully present and all ears. I don't know of anyone who listens as carefully or pays such close attention.

For years Jo has patiently entertained my struggling soliloquies about matters of my faith and heart. She's heard the details of almost every date I've ever had. For years she sensitively assured me that the nice guy who took me out for an expensive French dinner and never followed up with a phone call probably lost my number. And she still laughs about techno guy from our church who drove me to the middle of a public park and blasted Amy Grant's *Baby Baby* as a serenade from mountain-sized speakers that jutted out of the back of his pickup.

Jo not only heard about my dating escapades, she also compassionately listened to my struggles of faith. She's the one I told about my races around the rosary and the snooze button habit that prohibited precious morning quiet times of prayer and Bible reading. Jo was there for me when I was working out my faith. She bolstered me by listening to my life.

For years Jo's blue eyes have spoken compassion, grace, and welcome to me. And her ears—and heart—have listened to my stories. She has made an indelible mark on my life because of her *careful* listening. (And when I say careful, I mean full of caring.) She rarely gives advice or tries to fix my problems. She just looks me squarely in the eyes, focuses, pays attention, and offers a tissue when I need one.

Because of her integrity and investment in me, we maintain a friendship today, 20 years after our first meeting. In fact, we cheer each other on in our ministries. Jo continues to lead worship at a megachurch. She also travels internationally, teaching others about the ins and outs of meeting with God through worship.

When I think about Jo, read her writings in *Christianity Today,* or attend her conferences on worship, I understand why she's such an inviting listener. It's because she listens to God.

At one of her recent conferences, she said, "When I'm picking out music for a service, I often ask God, 'What do You want to hear, Father?' Then I sit quietly and wait to hear His answer. Usually it's an inaudible response. But I hear it, nevertheless."

Jo's fresh, daily conversational relationship with God is rare and ravishing. I'm glad she listens to God. And I'm forever grateful for all the years she has listened to me, too.

A friend is one before whom I may think aloud.

RALPH WALDO EMERSON

God Talk—God's Bent Ear

Give ear to my words, O LORD.

PSALM 5:1

I cried out to God with my voice...
and He gave ear to me.

PSALM 77:1 NKJV

Do we believe that God listens to us, like Jo listens to me? Is His ear really bent toward us? And if it is, does He attend to all of us...or just to a select, righteous few? Our answers to these questions greatly impact our prayer experience. If we don't think God is listening—and listening with care—our prayers are in vain. But if He hears, our prayers have eternal, essential, consequential, and vital value.

For decades I wondered if God listened to my prayers. When my requests for a husband went unanswered for years, I mistook His answer "to wait" for deafness. When I begged God to heal a broken relationship in my family, and the family members dug stubborn heels into the earth, I also perceived God as deaf. Even recently, when I prayed for a cure for my friend's sick daughter who ended up dying, I questioned God's wisdom and His willingness to listen and truly hear.

Wanting to know if God listens, I turned to my Bible on CD for answers. I started with a word search on "deaf." I anticipated finding verse after verse about God turning a deaf ear toward people like me who are selfish and imperfect. To my surprise, all of the verses I found on deafness referred to people—not God. Over and over, the prophets Isaiah and Jeremiah describe the Israelites—and us—as having lots of ear wax. Isaiah 48:8 and Jeremiah 17:23, 25:4, 34:14, and 44:16 list just a few of the examples I found. The gist of all of these verses is, and I paraphrase:

> God gave you one mouth and two ears. There-
> fore, you ought to listen twice as much as you

speak. But you don't. What's up, Israel/Sally? Do you have a bunch of cotton stuck in your ears?

I guess, because my ears are plugged so much of the time, I expected to have a God with earplugs. After reading repeatedly about my own inability to listen; I realized that I've been projecting my own clogged ears onto God!

Still, I wondered if there were "qualifiers" to being heard by God. I had a recollection of verses where God was ticked-off at Israel for being unrighteous. I remembered Him threatening to hide His face and stop answering prayers. On my Bible CD, I stumbled across one such verse in Micah 3:4. As it turns out, in this situation, God refused to listen because the religious leaders were practicing crude canni-balistic practices. Gladly, that's one way I'm not prone to offend God. So I continued my search for reasons God wouldn't hear my prayers.

I almost laughed out loud when I did a search on "ear" and came up with this: "Does he who implanted the ear not hear? Does he who formed the eye not see?" (Psalm 94:9). I love it! Of course God hears! Of course He sees! He made eyes. He made ears. He thought them up out of nothing. He's the celestial seer, the heavenly hearer. Nothing I say or do is out of His earshot.

Still my search was unquenched. I wanted to know if God specifically heard my prayers. So I imputed the word "hear" into my CD concordance. When the following verse appeared, I practically did a cartwheel: "Before they call I will answer; while they are still speaking I will hear" (Isaiah 65:24).

God does listen to us! And He listens with the relish and intensity of Jo. Why else would He answer *before* we call! He wants to know every detail of our days, every feeling of our hearts. He's so anxious to hear from us that He listens prior to and during our conversations. He's our parent. We're His kids.

God feels about us the way I feel about my children. When I pick the boys up from school, I eagerly await every detail of their day. I actually get a little rush of excitement when they tell me about the snacks they ate and who they played with in the gym. It thrills me to hear retellings of books they've been reading. I relish their artist commentaries on crafts they've made. And when they sing songs they've learned in music class my soul shimmers with joy. When my boys share, I savor every word.

God is our interested parent. As we go through our days, He's waiting with a bent ear to hear every detail of our lives. His face is turned toward us with inviting eyes and a compassionate smile. He wants to hear. He's poised and listening, waiting for questions, facts, struggles, joys, concerns, and requests.

Sometimes we misconstrue God's answers as an unwillingness to listen or an inability to hear. If God doesn't answer our prayers with a swift yes, we immediately jump to the conclusion that He's deaf. He isn't. He hears every word intently, savoring every morsel. He collects our tears in bottles. He cries when we cry. He jumps for joy when we succeed. Sometimes His answers to our prayers are "wait" or "no." But He still loves us and listens attentively.

Walking the Talk

I call on you, O God, for you will answer me;
give ear to me and hear my prayer.

PSALM 17:6

1. Consider the ways you listen to your friends, your family members, your spouse (if you're married). Are you a good listener? Write a journal entry about this.

2. Do you have a friend who is a particularly good listener? Call her and let her know how much you appreciate her listening ear.

3. How do you perceive God as a listener? Why? Take some time to think and pray about this. Then, if you have time, look up some of the verses referenced in this chapter and write down your new insights.

God, thanks for caring enough to hear and answer even before I call. Help me to listen like You do. Amen.

10

Empty to Fill

Prayers of Fasting

*Fasting helps us keep our balance in life.
How easily we begin to allow nonessen-
tials to take precedence in our lives. How
quickly we crave things we do not need
until we are enslaved by them.*[1]

RICHARD J. FOSTER

Girl Talk—Garage Sale Girlfriend

My friend Rachael is the garage sale queen. She doesn't *go*
to garage sales. She *has* them—at least one a year. Our group
of friends flocks to her sales. At them we've gleaned rugs,
mirrors, kitchenwares, children's toys, and much, much
more. Her sales are well-organized and well-planned. Her
driveway looks more like a department store than a flea
market on her sale days. The north side is devoted to household items; the south side is for clothing. The east end
houses a conglomeration of items her children have outgrown; the west end holds big, eye-catching items such as
old cribs, a baker's rack, and the treadmill that didn't do
much treading.

How does Rachael gather items for her sales? She is
addicted to spring cleaning...and she doesn't reserve it just
for the spring. She clears clutter from her home *all year long.*

Obsessive though she may be, I wish her household habits were contagious.

Unfortunately, I'm more of a collector than a cleaner. I regularly ask Rachael to come over and help me purge the junk I've accumulated. When I invite her over for a cleanout, she gets downright giddy. Usually she heads straight for my closet. This is painful because clothing has sentimental value to me. I hold onto almost every garment I've ever worn. I still have the dress I wore on my first date with Bryan and the pajamas I wore in the hospital after giving birth to our boys. I have sweaters from college, the outfit I donned on my first day as a *real* music teacher, and a costume from a play I was in during junior high.

Rachael respects my attachment to some of this apparel and has designated a special place in my closet for it. But she has no patience for the size eights that have hung unused for over five years (in the hope that I'll squeeze into them again). Anything that's obviously dated or hasn't been worn in over a year, she puts in a pile for Goodwill. Parting is sweet sorrow for me…but once I let go, I feel so much better!

Rachael doesn't stop with her home and my closet when it comes to purging. She also frequently cleans out the clutter of her life by turning off the TV for days at a time, giving up rich foods or white sugar for seasons, and curbing spending sprees. There's no doubt about it, Rachael is the queen of emptying herself in order to be filled in deeper ways.

When she and her family abstain from television, they play board games, take walks, and laugh more. When she turns off the car radio for weeks at a time, her kids start sharing secrets with her on the way to school and God meets with her on the way home. When she gives up sweets during Lent, she appreciates the Easter feast at her sister-in-law's with the intensity that only delayed gratification gives.

Rachael's food fasts, TV fasts, and clutter fasts open her home, body, and soul to live life fully and connect with God wholeheartedly in wide open spaces. Her plethora of fasts challenges me to consider all the distractions in my life that prevent strong connections with God. Seeing the benefits of fasting in her life, I'm challenged to fast, too.

It's because of Rach, that I've experienced two of my most meaningful fasts. The first took place a couple of Decembers ago. Following Rachael's example, I decided to fast from something that's very dear to me: writing. I vowed that instead of rushing through Christmas crafts, parties, and activities in order to get to my computer, I would take a little break from freelancing. It wasn't easy. But it was amazing. I was able to bake cookies with the boys, sing carols with my girlfriends, and drink eggnog while wrapping presents—all during hours I normally wrote. For once my holiday preparations during the most frenetic month of the year weren't rushed. And my soul had space to celebrate and prepare for Christ's birth in many meaningful and joyous and peaceful ways.

My December writing fast has become a tradition. I actually look forward to it. But boy was I in a panic when I got the contract for a book…and an impending deadline…in the middle of last December! I called Rachael and told her of my predicament. She assured me that the purpose of fasting is to empty myself in order to be filled, not to be traumatized or tortured. Rachael extended to me the liberty to break my writing fast. Under that grace, I found freedom. I ended up continuing the fast because I *wanted* to—not because I *had* to. Grace upon grace, the book was completed on time, and my family enjoyed a most festive and restorative Advent.

The other memorable fast I've experienced because of Rachael took place last summer. For this fast, Rachael and I abstained from food for a day in order to pray for a mutual friend whose baby daughter had died. We were unable to attend the out-of-state funeral, but we used our hunger pangs as reminders to pray for healing, hope, and comfort. As we emptied ourselves, God met us and we sensed that He was with our dear friend, too. When we broke the fast, we shared a light meal and sang hymns of praise for fullness in Christ.

Our seasons of fasting and prayer at the Tabernacle have been high days indeed; never has Heaven's gate stood wider; never have our hearts been nearer the central Glory.[2]

C.H. SPURGEON

God Talk—The Emptied Christ

Jesus, full of the Holy Spirit, returned from the Jordan and was led by the Spirit in the desert, where for forty days he was tempted by the devil. He ate nothing during those days, and at the end of them he was hungry.

LUKE 4:1-2

Jesus is a lot like my friend Rachael. He often put things aside in order to make room to see, know, hear, and commune with God. He fasted at the onset of His ministry, He fasted during His ministry, and He fasted through His death. Really, if you think about it, Jesus' *entire life* was a kind of fast.

We all know the story of Jesus' baptism by John the Baptist. Jesus goes down to the Jordan where many people are getting dunked. The Spirit of God is in the water and the sky. No one really notices it, though, until a carpenter's son from Galilee gets into the mucky current. When Jesus wades into the water and is submerged by John, the sky cracks in two. A dove flies down and lands on Jesus' head. As if that isn't enough, God's voice descends, too. He says (and I paraphrase), "Jesus is My kid. I'm proud of Him. I love Him to the moon and back."

This moment in the Jordan marks the beginning of Jesus' ministry. It is an extremely intimate and powerful moment. So it's hard to believe that after this public blessing, Jesus would need to get any closer to God. But for 40 days He goes into the desert and fasts. He eats absolutely nothing in order to spiritually feast on God. Just like Rachael, He empties Himself in order to be filled with God.

At the height of His hunger, the devil tempts Him to turn a stone into a baguette. And believe me, He could've done it. But instead, Jesus allows the fast to teach something He already knows: We do not live on bread alone. (It's a good thing that it wasn't me in the desert with a growling stomach. I've never met a carb I didn't like. And there's no way I could've passed up a loaf of bread after 40 days without food.)

Thankfully, Jesus was more disciplined than I am. As a result, His 40-day fast fortified Him for the work of ministry He was to do for the rest of His life. Ironically, instead of becoming weak from the fast, Jesus received spiritual strength for the tasks ahead. He learned from this desert experience. And any time Jesus needed renewed strength or connection with God, He withdrew from the crowds, emptied Himself, and was filled with communion with God.

An example of this occurs after Jesus feeds a picnic to more than 5,000 people and before He walks on water. Jesus has just given the gift of a miraculous multiplying meal, along with a message of mercy. After this, John tells that the people wanted to make Him a king. Instead of basking in the glory of the moment, Jesus goes up to a mountainside to be alone and pray. He fasts from the praise of people. He abstains from accolades. He empties Himself of things that could diminish His connection with God.

Being an extrovert, I find this hard to grasp. Jesus' actions run against my grain. If I had done a miracle of that proportion, I would have hung around to bask in the glory. I would've welcomed the crown, the purple robe, the laurels, and the praise. I would have magnified myself and diminished God instead of the reverse. Jesus didn't. He declined. He met with His Father on a mountaintop to revel in true glory.

Jesus dispensed of Himself even in death. He died on a cross, sandwiched between two common, cussing robbers. Instead of avoiding the cross to preserve pride, long life, and honor, He "gave up his spirit" (John 19:30). His spirit was all He had left. And He even let that go. When He did, Jesus became the fulfillment of His own words, "Blessed are the poor in spirit, for theirs is the kingdom of heaven" (Matthew 5:3).

Jesus' death is the perfect metaphor for His entire life. Over and over He gave up His spirit. He poured Himself out like Mary poured the perfume. He was a valuable, expensive gift, abundantly broken and spilled...emptied.

Often I think about the life and death of Christ. I compare His life to mine. When I do, I wonder if Jesus missed the things after which I strive. The things I think will fill me: a spouse, a home, security, accolades, achievements.

I wonder if Jesus might've wanted a wife, someone with whom He could share daily life and a bed...someone He could kiss good night. But He abdicated this pleasure. Instead, Jesus was given true friendship in Mary Magdalene, Lazarus, Mary and Martha, a crew of 12 goofy fishermen, and others. And, ultimately, *God* became His companion, His spouse.

I also wonder if Jesus might've wanted a home, an abode with comfortable chairs and a pillow for His head...a place where the newspaper would come in the morning and the porch swing would creak on Sundays. But He emptied Himself of that comfort, too. He was a homeless man who was given the spare rooms of friends and spots by a sky-clad campfire to rest and sup. And He knew that God was His eternal home.

I wonder if Jesus wanted security and predictability? A reliable job with health insurance, a retirement plan...and maybe even a 401k. But He willingly relinquished this for a wild and wondrous life, a life where God became His true security.

Jesus' practical life and prayer life are mirrors for each other. In both He forsook Himself in order to make more room for God. Let's follow His example, and the example of Rachael. When we're tempted to fill our lives with sounds and stuff, let's stop and listen. Then we can rid ourselves of things that will not truly fill us and be satisfied with the richest of fare. Isn't it ironic that as we fast and pray, we'll actually "taste and see that the LORD is good" (Psalm 34:8)?

Walking the Talk

*Many of the great Christians throughout church
history fasted and witnessed to its value; among
them were Martin Luther, John Calvin, John Knox,
John Wesley, Jonathan Edwards, David Brainerd,
Charles Finney and Pastor His of China.*[3]

RICHARD J. FOSTER

1. Consider fasting. You may decide to fast from food or you may want to fast from spending, television, talking, listening to music, sexual activity (with the consent of your spouse), reading, writing, or other activities. Start with a day or half a day. Then consider extending the time to a day or two. (Please note: If you're planning an extended fast from food, you should probably consult a doctor first. Also, consult Richard J. Foster's *Celebration of Discipline*. It includes a great chapter on fasting.)

2. Think about ways you can clean out the clutter in your life in order to make room for God. Maybe it's time to clean out your closet or have a garage sale. Notice the life metaphors of emptying to be filled.

3. Ask a friend to join you in a time of fasting and prayer. Break your fast together with a light meal and a time of praise.

Lamb of God, thank You for emptying Yourself, being broken and spilled out for me. Help me follow Your example as I let go of things that have their claws in me. Amen.

11

I Think I'll Go for a Walk Outside

Experiencing Prayer in Nature

> *This is my Father's world, and to my listening ears all nature sings, and round me rings the music of the spheres.... This is my Father's world, the birds their carols raise, the morning light, the lily white, declare their Maker's praise.*
>
> MALTBIE D. BABCOCK

Girl Talk—Hannah, My Outdoorsy Girlfriend

Hannah loves nature. Her birthday's in the fall, and on her special day, all she ever wants for a gift is the luxury to go on a walk and take in the colors of turning leaves. Often Hannah tells me she feels closest to God in nature. She says, "Sal, God talks to me in all the things I see on my walks."

"I guess I can imagine experiencing God's majesty in a mountain," I say, "or seeing His beauty in a sunset." But I have a feeling Hannah experiences something *deeper* when she converses with the Creator of the universe. I think she feels God's touch in gentle breezes. She experiences the colors of His love on her walk through autumn leaves of gold, crimson, and orange. She senses His power in the crash of Lake Michigan's waves.

One day Hannah and I were having a "play date." We sat in her kitchen sipping Vanilla Nut Decaf. Our children ran around playing cowboys and Indians in her basement. We started talking about the ways God speaks to us through nature. I told her that I just didn't quite get it. And that God's voice is usually clearest to me when I sit in my overstuffed chair with a Bible and a Mozart CD. Before I knew it, Hannah had all four of our kids bundled in hooded sweatshirts and scarves. She and I donned our most comfortable walking shoes and hit the trail in a nearby forest preserve. We ended up pulling our kids in red wagons on a hike that lasted more than an hour.

The trees arched overhead like an autumnal quilt. The ground looked as if it were covered by the Quilter's colorful fabric scraps. We crunched our feet in the bits and pieces of yellow, red, and green. And for the first time I began to hear God whisper—through nature—to my heart. As I shuffled through the crunchy colors, it seemed as if God was trying to tell me something. Perhaps the message was that He'd take all the unmatched tattered pieces of my life and stitch them together with a strand of love and creativity. This was the first of many nature walks Hannah and I have since taken with our kids.

Last spring we took another walk. It was during that walk that I began to truly hear God's voice speaking through creation the way Hannah does. My eyes and ears were finally opening because she, and the children, led the way. Children are normally curious. They pick up, smell, explore, and notice just about everything. On our walk this time, we didn't bring wagons, and the children bounced about the wooded path like a litter of snoopy puppies. They eagerly explored the grounds, bringing back rocks, feathers, sticks, and other treasures for show-and-tell along the way.

At one point my son, Ben, retrieved the remains of two bright blue robin's eggs. Hannah's daughter discovered an empty, torn chrysalis. "What a fragile home," she said, amazing us with her poetic heart. Nearing the end of the path, Hannah's son, Max, yelled, "Guys, check this out!"

We walked to the edge of the path where Max stooped over, pointing to a little sprout of green emerging from the earth. "Look," he said. "A maple tree is starting to grow, and the seed pod's still attached to it."

We all bent over, and sure enough the miniature green sapling was topped by a broken seed pod. The sprout looked as if it were wearing an Easter bonnet.

On our way back to the car we deeply took in our last few breaths of fresh air. The sun began to set, and the sky broke open, spilling out pink, tangerine, and lavender. Ayden, my youngest son, kicked a rock. It was round, gray, and bumpy.

"Hold on a second, Ayden," said Hannah. "I think the rock you're kickin' might be a geode. Let's take it home, smack it a few times with a hammer, and find out."

Ayden picked up the rock and cradled it in his lap like a baby the whole way home in the car. When we got to Hannah's, the group gathered on her front porch. With a sledgehammer, Hannah whacked the rock three times. Under the third powerful whack, the rock yielded, rending in two. Sparkly crystals seemed to explode from the rock like fireworks. The children were awestruck.

We sat on the front step passing the glistening geode halves around and around. "I think God was talking to us today, guys," Hannah said with a casual, cheerful tone. "What do you think He was saying?"

Silence fell from a lack of answers. Then Hannah said, "Let's try to think of all the things we saw in nature today: a broken robin's egg, a shattered chrysalis, the sunset, a seed-pod hat, and this geode. Is there something all these things have in common?"

"They're all broken!" said Ayden jumping up and down with the joy of his answer.

"That's absolutely right," said Hannah smiling and patting Ayden on the shoulder. "Everything we saw was broken. The egg broke to let out a baby bird. The chrysalis ripped for a butterfly to emerge. The geode cracked, revealing sparkles. The seed cracked for the tree to sprout. Even the sky broke open, letting us see the colors of the sunset. Maybe God is trying to tell us something. Maybe He's saying that beauty grows out of brokenness."

In that moment the children and I heard the voice of God in a loud, clear, and vivid prayer that we'll never forget.

This is my Father's world: He shines in all that's fair;
in the rustling grass, I hear Him pass;
He speaks to me everywhere.

MALTBIE D. BABCOCK

God Talk—It Is Good!

The heavens are telling of the glory of God.

PSALM 19:1 NASB

God, like Hannah, loves nature. One of the ways He speaks to His people is through natural revelation. Simply put, God talks to us through the things He has made.

What cracks me up about this is that God used *words* to make the world. In Genesis, it says that He *spoke* the world into existence. Then, strangely enough, He chooses to speak to us through nature *without* words. What a funny paradox! Picture it. God speaks creation into being. All He has to do is *say the word,* and the world is. He isn't bound by the convention of creating with hands, as humans are.

Carpenters measure and cut boards. Then they nail them together to form mantels, walls, and steps. Writers pound away at computers, using brains and fingers to create sentences and chapters. Bakers labor in kitchens mixing eggs, milk, butter, sugar, and flour to make cakes. God is above this. "By the *word of the* LORD were the heavens made, their starry host by the breath of his mouth....For he *spoke,* and it came to be" (Psalm 33:6,9). I don't care how talented a carpenter, writer, or baker is at her craft. There's no way she can "speak or breathe" a creation into being. And even if a carpenter could speak stairs into space; a writer could will words into a manuscript; or a baker could tell a torte to tower—there's absolutely no way any of them could make stars, firmaments, universes.

God is so mighty and magical! He *speaks* an inconceivable, immense, intricate, complicated creation into being simply with *words.* Then He uses that creation to *speak* to us nonverbally. God's communication is so creative it makes me smile. Isn't it amazing that we can hear His voice in glaciers and galaxies, starfish and sunsets? We really can...if we listen in unexpected places.

Most of us are not used to listening for God's words through acorns, seashells, ladybugs, or hillsides. In fact, most of us are not that good at listening at all. But listening is a huge part of praying, even though it's often overlooked.

I wonder, sometimes, if God chooses to speak in unconventional ways (like through nature) because we're not very good listeners. He's dying to get our attention, dying to tell us of His love. Over and over, in the Gospels, Jesus repeats "[She] who has ears, let [her] hear." And over and over again, the people of first-century Palestine fail to listen, to understand, to hear the words of God. We're a lot like them.

For centuries, God has been begging for us to *listen*. He sends life-giving messages through the world and through His words. Of course He communicates through written and spoken words found in the Bible, the mouths of our friends, priests, pastors, the pens of writers, leaders, theologians, through literature, poetry, and song lyrics and so forth. And when we miss or are unable to hear all of this, He's still there providing an unavoidable way of keeping in touch.

Through nature, something we come in contact with every day, God is talking to us. He's heard when we drive our kids to school, when we look out the window by our desk, and when the paper moon rises and lemony sun sets every evening. When we don't, or can't, listen to spoken words, God is creative enough to give an alternate way of hearing Him: through willows and wasps, giraffes and geodes.

How wonderful is God? He meets us, in prayer, through things wild, wonderful, and ineffable. He teaches us about Himself. And He provides a variety of ways for us to communicate and commune with the one who hung the stars in space. In response, let us listen, with Hannah, to His multicolored voice.

Fair are the meadows,
Fairer still the woodlands,
Robed in the blooming garb of spring;
Jesus is fairer, Jesus is purer,
Who makes the woeful heart to sing.

Fair is the sunshine,
Fairer still the moonlight,
And all the twinkling starry host;
Jesus shines brighter, Jesus shines purer
Than all the angels heaven can boast.

GERMAN JESUITS
Fairest Lord Jesus

Walking the Talk

Our world is saturated with grace, and the
lurking presence of God is revealed not only in
spirit but in matter—in a deer leaping across a
meadow, in the flight of an eagle, in fire and
water, in a rainbow after a summer storm,...in
Beethoven's Ninth Symphony, in a child licking a
chocolate ice cream cone, in a woman with
windblown hair. God intended for us to discover
His loving presence in the world around us.[1]

BRENNAN MANNING

We must rediscover the gospel of grace
and the world of grace.[2]

BRENNAN MANNING

1. Take a nature walk. As you walk, look and listen for God's voice.

2. Collect an object from nature: a seashell, a rock, a leaf, a branch, a flower, or a feather. Sit on a park bench and examine the object. Ask God to reveal something about Himself to you through the object.

3. Watch the sunset tonight. Thank God for the beauty of the earth and the beauty of Himself.

Creator, what You've made is radiant, intricate, and dazzling to my eyes. It all reflects Your immense beauty. Thank You for talking to me through cumulous clouds, caterpillars, crashing waves, and cardinals. May I hear with capable, intent fingers, ears, nose, and eyes. Amen.

12

Turkeys, Yule Logs, Christmas Trees, and Stars

Tradition and Symbol as Prayer

> *Around the table we sit, as the candles*
> *flicker and burn down. We share ideas.*
> *We share food...Love. Inclusion...Lamb*
> *and potatoes. Bread and wine. Enjoyed*
> *together, in the understanding that all*
> *of life is a sacrament.*[1]
>
> MADELEINE L'ENGLE

Girl Talk—Lainey's House of Church

Whenever I go to Lainey's house, I know immediately what season or holiday she is celebrating with her family. During Eastertide, Lainey's table is lined with lilies as white as doves. Their sweet aroma reminds me of the risen Christ. The decaying bulbs, yielding tall green stems and glorious flowers remind me of life being born out of death. At Christmas each year, Lainey has a freshly cut Scotch pine decked in red and white. It's a constant reminder of communication between heaven and earth as its roots once reached into the ground and its branches point toward God.

Lainey's decorations are just ordinary things, but they're filled with deep spiritual meanings. They cycle with the seasons: gourds and apples, ceramic turkeys, a crèche, a wooden cross, Easter eggs, flags.

Her décor is not Martha Stewart or over-the-top in any way. At the same time, Lainey's embellishments are joyful, not junky. They're simple and celebratory. Lainey has a special closet where she keeps all of her revolving ornaments. Housed in one location, they're easy to get at and needn't be replaced from year to year. With an organized, easy system like this, she's able to focus more on the reasons for the seasons and less on the preparations.

I like being at Lainey's anytime, but I especially enjoy being there during times of festivity. During November, as we anticipate Thanksgiving, Lainey has guests trace their hands on a huge chalkboard that hangs in her family room. Then she asks them to draw bird legs, waddles, eyes, and beaks on their tracings—turning them into turkeys. Each finger of the hand-birds represents a feather. On the finger-feathers, she encourages guests to write things for which they're thankful. By Thanksgiving Day, the board is jam-packed with dozens of written thanksgiving prayers.

During Advent and Christmas, Lainey also has abundant symbols and traditions. Many a year, I've had the honor of hiding baby Jesus with Lainey's girls. We've found great places: in teapots, behind books, in a cookie jar, under the Christmas tree. Then on Christmas day, the girls' daddy has to hunt and find the babe. When he does, the family breaks into a jubilant rendition of "Happy birthday to You, Baby Jesus!" And, another prayer of praise is raised.

After Christmas, Lainey's husband, Peter, cuts the branches from the tree. Then he saws the trunk in half, and nails it together creating a cross. The cross is displayed in the dining room during Lent. Ultimately, it becomes the next year's yule log, and is burned in a Christmastide fire. As it burns, it offers the perfect symbol for all the prayer offerings that have risen, like smoke, from Lainey's home during the past year. And it reminds Lainey's family of another cycle of faith beginning, once again, with the birth of the Christ child.

The twelfth day following Christmas, Lainey commemorates the visit of the Wise Men to baby Jesus in Bethlehem. She does this with a star-studded meal. She hangs glittering stars from her chandelier and sets her table with star-shaped plates and bowls. Then she warms soup with star noodles, freezes star-shaped ice cubes, and bakes star cookies. As Lainey and her loved ones eat, drink, and talk, candles burn brightly on the table—miniature reminders of the Star of Bethlehem. Lainey's family remember the story of the gift-bearing trip made by three ancient kings. And they thank the One True King for giving the Perfect Gift.

Epiphany comes from the Greek word that means "showing." It's funny, but I seem to have many spiritual epiphanies at Lainey's house. Her traditions and symbols have been showing God to her husband and children...and me...for years. We've seen God's abundant provision in Thanksgiving turkeys, God's unexpected gifts in a Christmas crèche, and resurrection life in lilies. With each new season, Lainey's stellar rituals create fresh ways for us to see God and to pray.

When I check my view from the tightrope, I spot angels appearing in both icons and syndicated comic strips; discern spiritual significance in homemade soup; and find Indiana Jones rubbing elbows with St. Ephraim the Syrian.[2]

DONNA FARLEY

God Talk—God's House

*The liturgical seasons are all about
"the Church at prayer."*[3]
DENNIS J. BILLY

*Most people understand imagery and symbol
better than doctrine and dogma.*[4]
BRENNAN MANNING

The house of God is the local church. It's filled with traditions and symbols—just like Lainey's house. Whether your church is small and in the country or if it's a cathedral with heaven-high spires, inside you'll find bread and wine, water and oil, ashes and palms, mangers and crosses, candles and incense. God's decorative symbols and icons are abundant. They fill His houses in pictures, books, tapestries, sculptures, altars, and stained-glass windows. All of these decorations, along with festive banners and seasonal floral arrangements, welcome God's family to times of fasting and feasting alike.

Let's imagine what it'd be like to be a daughter in God's house for a year. It's four weeks before Christmas: Advent. God sits on the altar steps with you. He's wearing a violet robe. Beside Him is an empty manger. He offers you a glass of wine and some crusty French bread. You take it.

"What do you want for Christmas?" He asks, sliding closer to you.

You rest your head on His shoulder and reluctantly rattle off a list.

God listens intently. Then He stands up and walks around the manger three times. It looks a lot like the altar behind it. Wooden. Bare. Open.

"Why is there a manger in your living room?" you ask.

"It's here as a decoration—a reminder that Christmas is coming." God looks into the manger as if He sees something beautiful and pleasing, something wondrous.

You get up and look, too. But there's nothing inside except wood shavings and straw. In a split second, the manger becomes a window. You peer into it and see emptiness. It reminds you of the vacant crib waiting in the nursery of your home when you were expecting your first child. It reminds you of the crèche your mother set under your Christmas tree every year, awaiting a miniature baby Jesus. It reminds you of all the things you're waiting for: a word from the doctor, a call about that new job, a note from a friend you terribly miss.

God knows what you're thinking. He wraps a strong, warm arm around your shoulders and draws you to Himself. "Waiting can be difficult," He says. "But living in times of advent can be good when you realize that Christmas is always around the corner."

About five months later, God invites you to a dinner at His house. You wear your favorite dress and Manolo Blahnik heels. He serves lamb and potatoes, bread and wine. He's wearing a red robe this time. You've never seen Him look sad before, but the corners of His eyes look pink and He seems to have a stuffy nose. You offer Him a Kleenex. He takes it.

The food is delicious. You devour it. But He hardly eats. God smiles gently at you. He puts down His fork and knife. Then a solitary tear bumps down His wrinkled cheek like a boulder down a mountain. You notice that the cross hanging behind His dining room table is covered in a black veil. It occurs to you that this dinner party is more of a funeral than a feast.

You realize that it's Good Friday. Jesus' journey from Galilee to Jerusalem flashes in your memory. You think about the life and death journeys in your own life. Your marriage. Then the divorce. The pregnancy. Then the miscarriage. God hugs you. You hug Him back.

"Come back on Sunday," He says softly, "and wear white."

You put on a flower-kissed bonnet and a white taffeta dress for church on Sunday. God wears white, too. You deeply inhale the intoxicating aroma of Easter lilies. He smiles as big as the horizon.

"Christ is risen!" He shouts with a rumbling resonance that shakes the altar.

"He is risen indeed!" you joyously yell in reply.

As this scene makes clear, God walks with us through the holidays and seasons of our lives. He uses traditions to help us stay connected. And when words aren't enough, He uses symbols to "speak." God knows symbols help us see, touch, taste, hear, smell...to experience. He knows that through our five senses we can clearly communicate and commune. All we have to do is look at pictures, feel holy oil on our foreheads, taste communion bread, light candles, smell incense, or get wet with the waters of baptism and we're talking with God.

It's one thing to say, "I believe Christ will sustain me." But when we actually put a piece of communion bread in our mouth, chew and swallow, we experience what we believe. As we taste and digest the bread, we have a sensory experi-

ence. We actually take *God in*; we feel Him filling and satis-
fying us. Our actions become a prayer that's deeply sensual.

God's symbols don't merely apply to pious concepts.
Though they may be rooted in spiritual truths, they also contain extremely personal messages. Remember Lainey's lilies?
Their spiritual truth was that life comes after death. So their
personal promise is that we have hope after loss: healing
after a divorce, adoption after infertility, second chances after
unemployment, joy out of depression.

If we listen to our lives with eyes, ears, fingers, mouths,
and noses, we'll hear God communicating truths through
symbols. We can listen at church, and we can listen in the
homes of our friends. God's symbols are everywhere.
They're as earthy, organic, and common as bread and water,
light and darkness, apples and snakes.

God wants to connect with us in holy and human ways,
so He provides symbols and traditions, the way Lainey does,
as reminders to stay in touch during the dailiness of life. As
we interact with crosses and candles, dinners and deaths,
water and wine, births and bread, hopefully we'll see new
ways of praying during all the seasons of our lives.

*I have learned a great deal about...praying spontaneously
and immediately, from my evangelical friends, and this is
a lesson I treasure. Some of my friends have learned
something about symbols as open windows to God
from me and other sacramentalists.*[5]

MADELEINE L'ENGLE

Walking the Talk

The beauty of the Church seasons is that they teach us how to balance our life. The succession of feast and fast tells us that God does not demand either too much of us, or too little. The Christian life is a whole life, an expansive life, a life in Christ, who gives Himself for the life of the world.[6]

DONNA FARLEY

1. Do you decorate for holidays? What decorations do you use and why?

   Did your family of origin decorate the home for special occasions?

   Write a journal entry about one or both of these questions.

2. Think about the significance of traditions and symbols in your home. Are there any you would like to continue, add, or change? Implement your thoughts!

3. Are you in a time of Advent (waiting), Christmastide (rejoicing), Lent (emptiness), or Eastertide (new birth) right now? Why? How can you embrace this season? Journal about this.

4. If you do not have a lot of meaningful symbols in your home, consider taking a trip to your local Christian bookstore or a craft store. Choose something that will serve as a reminder that your life is a prayer through the seasons.

Great God, thank You for seasons and symbols. May crosses and crèches, candles and cornucopias, help me connect with You in tangible reality. Amen.

Zimbabwe, China, Afghanistan, and Brazil

Loving the World in Prayer

*I looked and there before me was a great multitude
that no one could count, from every nation,
tribe, people and language, standing
before the throne and in front of the Lamb...
And they cried out in a loud voice:
Salvation belongs to our God....*

REVELATION 7:9-10

Girl Talk—Jules, the World Traveler

Because of a computer-related job, my friend Jules has traveled around the globe. No matter where she goes she says that after a while it starts feeling like home away from home. She's so different from me. When I travel, I freak out about strange bathrooms. I worry about getting lost. I have anxiety about language, fearing that I'll get tongue-tied or say something offensive if I try to speak Chinese or Spanish or German.

When I was a teenager, I remember trying to express my embarrassment to some Spanish-speaking friends. When I used the word "embarazada," they erupted in laughter. Because of a poor verb choice, I had mistakenly announced that I was *pregnant*. Clearly I'm not the most cross-culturally savvy person. Unfortunately, I live a comfortable life within the stifling security of local language, common customs, and the familiar foods of my native home. These comforts high-light my apprehensions about worldwide wanderings.

Jules, on the other hand, delights in world safaris. She enjoys exploring unknown territories, tasting new spicy or exotic food, trying out new dances and rituals. She's sensitive to other cultures. At the same time, she's unafraid to take risks or be embarrassed by faux pas. She plunges deeply into the customs of whatever land she's in, embracing new ways, new people, and new things.

Over the years, Jules has collected hundreds of souvenirs from her journeys. Her home looks like a world museum. From Africa, she has masks of the Ashanti people. They hang in a grouping above her fireplace mantel. Below them, on the coffee table, is a woven basket. Its geometric pattern looks like a circle of Zs that remind Jules of Zimbabwe. Her Djembe drum, beside the couch, is yet another reminder.

Jules' guest room is in homage to China. The décor is a collage of red and gold with hints of black. A scroll calligraphy painting hangs above the bed, and a collection of porcelain vases line a shellacked angular dresser. Swords from the Panjiayuan Market in Bejing rest on a rack by the door. And a tower of Chinese chests and baskets graces one of the room's corners.

Every inch of Jules' house has a geographic theme. My favorite is her Brazilian bathroom. Above her toilet is a colorful oil on canvas by Claudia Cseri. It's of a woman with long black hair. She looks as if she's emerging from a forest of geometric shapes in yellow, peach, and orange. On the sink is a pair of pewter candlesticks and a pewter bowl, all from Brazil. Complementing them is a bright blue Monte Sião pitcher.

At Jules' home, I feel like I'm taking a mini trip around the world. When I ask her which souvenir is her favorite, she says, "The best mementos I've ever brought back with me are the friendships I've made."

As proof, Jules has a big black album filled with pictures in which she's hugging international friends. Photo after photo shows her red hair and fair skin contrasting with the faces of friends of all shades and colors. The pictures catalog a rainbow of friendship gathered over years of travel. Along with the pictures, Jules has letters, postcards, matchbooks, hotel receipts, and other paper trinkets from around the globe. Their colors and diversity also complement the beauty and uniqueness of her friends' faces.

The album sits on a well-cushioned ottoman in her great room. I think it's symbolic that Jules keeps this book in the most warm, comfortable, familial room of her house. It echoes the standing welcome and love Jules has in her heart for global friends.

Often when I visit Jules, we sit with hazelnut coffee and look through her album. She tells me tales of travels and anecdotes about amigos. Inevitably we end up praying for her faraway friends. It's funny, but when we pray, her friends become my friends. Instead of feeling foreign, unfamiliar, and a world a way, they feel as if they're sitting on the couch with us. After we pray I usually feel a kindred spirit with the world that I never could have imagined without Jules.

Though I may not ever be as comfortable with world travel as she is, Jules has taught me that there is beauty in diversity. And no matter how many differences people have, we're all a lot alike. We all have hopes and hurts and longing hearts. And most importantly, we're all God's beloved children.

Red and yellow, black and white,
They are precious in His sight,
Jesus loves the little children of the world.[1]

God Talk—The Lover of the World

For God so loved the world that he gave his one
and only Son, that whoever believes in him shall
not perish but have eternal life.

JOHN 3:16

Knowing Jules has helped me understand a new dimension of John 3:16, the famous verse many have memorized or seen held up on placards in the stands at baseball games: "For God so loved the world...." When I think about God *loving the world,* it seems impersonal or general. But when I picture God, like Jules, sitting with a family photo album, looking at His children, I understand the kind of love about which John writes.

Interestingly enough, John writes about God's immense love in his Gospel the book of John. Then, in Revelation, he writes about God *with* a book: the Book of Life. John describes God sitting on a white throne among many open books (Revelation 20:12). I like to imagine that God's books are a lot like Jules' scrapbook. And I like to picture the throne as an oversized rocking chair.

I see God like an affectionate mother rocking in His chair, treasuring memories of each of His children on planet Earth. He lingers over their photos and writes fond stories about them in His books. They're like Creative Memory albums made by the Creator—imagine that!

One of His open books holds a picture of Mei from Yangjiang, China. She is three months old. Her eyes sparkle with tears. Her mouth is wide with a cry. She's bundled in a basket beneath a tattered blanket. Two pink fists gripping the rag look like rosebuds beside her face. Beneath the photo, God has inscribed: *I see you Mei. And I love you. Though your mommy had to abandon you, she loves you, too! Remember, My dear one, that I will never leave or forsake you.*

Another open scrapbook compiled by the Creator reveals a picture of a couple from Sri Lanka. In one photo their eyes are tired, but they beam with elation. The man proudly holds a new baby boy—his first son. In a later picture, the husband and wife sit on a tsunami-ravaged beach with searching terror in their eyes.

Next to their pictures, God has written: *Parents of Ramanathan. I was overjoyed at the birth of your baby. And now I cry with you at his absence from your lives. I will hold Ramy, and you, in the palm of My hand until, once again, you are united.*

Millions of memory books lay open surrounding God's rocker. I see Jules' album, my husband's, Cheri's, three for her children, three for mine. Margaret's is there. So is Hannah's and her children's...and yours. The faces in the photos look like the faces in Jules' album: lovely, diverse, multicolored, multicultural.

At another point in the book of Revelation, John writes that we will all stand before God's almighty rocking chair: "There before me was a great multitude...from every nation, tribe, people and language, standing before the throne" (Revelation 7:9). Together, as one big happy family, we hang out with God. And He promises that "never again will [we] hunger," and that He will "wipe away every tear from [our] eyes" (Revelation 7:16-17). All of the children in God's photo album together with their Father forever. No more tsunamis, no more tears, no more abandonment. Just togetherness and peace.

With this image in my mind, and the images in Jules' scrapbook, I realize that as daughters of God, we're all connected. We are *all* God's children. God has adopted us. He has made us part of a family that extends beyond geographic and racial boundaries. Because of this, we are compelled to love the world and pray for healing and blessings in our international family.

Our prayer lives could get really boring if we only supplicated and interceded on behalf of ourselves and our immediate friends and family. How exciting to be able to branch out and pray for the world! The evening news, newspapers, and international websites list details about national disasters, personal tragedies, cultural wars, lost orphans, and others who are poor and needy. These resources can become our enlarged, others-centered prayer lists.

We don't have to be world travelers like Jules to love and pray for our brothers and sisters. All we have to do is open our eyes and ears to the needs of our global family...and pray.

*In this day, when tribalism sparks massacres in Africa,
when nations redraw boundaries based on ethnic
background, when racism in the United States mocks our
nation's great ideals...I know of no more powerful message
of the gospel than this....The walls separating us from each
other...have been demolished...God loves us....*[2]

PHILIP YANCEY

Walking the Talk

*Just as the pieces of the quilt are sewn together
with interlocking stitches, all people are linked
together in the fabric of our world. In a way, the
patchwork quilt represents all the different people
of the world. We are individual in our attitudes,
lifestyles, and backgrounds, yet we share so
much of what it means to be human.*[3]

TERESA GUSTAFSON

1. Start a new prayer journal. Use it to pray for your international sisters and brothers.

2. If you have traveled abroad, share your stories. Educate your friends about the people you know and love from faraway places. If you aren't a seasoned traveler, ask a friend who travels to share her tales of travel with you.

3. Select a world cause, and commit to pray for it for a given period of time (a week, a month, a year). Ask God how

you can be an agent of healing to global sisters and brothers.

Father of the world, thank You for my international brothers and sisters. Remind me to pray for them often and with compassion. Amen.

Love in Any Language

Prayer as the Speech of the Heart

*During that semester there was a volatility
to the written language; it constantly shifted
in my eyes, and each day the shapes
became something other than what they
had been before. Spoken Chinese was also
starting to settle in my ears, and soon I
could make simple conversation.*[1]

PETER HESSLER

Girl Talk—Chinese 101 with Millie

"Wan shang hao. Wo shi Millie. Huan ying nin!" Those were the first words I heard in my Conversational Chinese class taught by my friend Millie. Translation: "Good evening. I am Millie. Welcome!" I took the class at a local college because I wanted to have a few Mandarin words under my belt before Bryan and I traveled to China to adopt our little girl.

The class was difficult. Learning any new language can be tough. "Mandarin Chinese [has] a reputation as a difficult language—some experts say it takes four times as long to learn as Spanish or French—and its characters and tones are particularly challenging to a Westerner because they are completely different from the way our languages are structured."[2]

My favorite part of the class was listening to Millie and her friend Ping read the dialogues in our textbook. As I listened in, it was difficult to believe that the women were actually conversing. But they were. Their voices lilted through the lines like a lover reading a sonnet. But when I read, the dialogues sounded more like silverware being dropped on a tile floor.

Many times after class Millie, Ping, and I went out for tea. Every now and then I'd catch them candidly conversing in Chinese. Watching their animated facial expressions and noticing their body language, I recognized that Chinese felt as normal and natural to them as English did to me. This should have been *obvious*. But the stilted, staccato tones threw me off. Even though I wanted to embrace this foreign language as a way of connecting to China and my little girl, it was "other," alien and exotic.

The class lasted only 12 weeks—not nearly long enough. When it was over, though I was far from mastering conversational Chinese, I had gained a friend in Millie. And I had learned the most important phrase I'll probably ever say in Mandarin: "Ni hao. Wo shi Ma Ma. Wo ai ni." Translation: "Hi. I'm your Mom. I love you." I'm glad to have learned these words and a few others. Still, I realize that given my hideous accent and limited vocabulary, our daughter is more likely to understand my feelings for her simply by the body language of love that I'll exhibit when I hold her for the first time.

Millie continues to tutor me in Chinese these days. My mom and I are currently taking a private Chinese Calligraphy class from her. For several weeks we had to paint spots. Then it was lines. This week we wrote our first words: yi, er, san (one, two, three). Millie is patient with us. We're slow learners.

The process is arduous because we're as awkward with our brush strokes as I was with my tongue and the tones. Thank goodness for Millie's constant reminders: "first tone, straight, straight…budui! (incorrect!)…second tone, down to up…dui! (correct!)" My pursuit of linguistic study is slowly progressing. Often I wonder how it makes Millie feel to hear me mangle her native tongue. When I worry about that, I find comfort that my friend knows the language of my heart.

Isn't it funny the way some combinations of words can give you—almost apart from their meaning— a thrill like music?[3]

C.S. LEWIS

God Talk—Linguist of the Heart

With your blood you purchased men for God from every tribe and language and people and nation. You have made them to be a kingdom and priests to serve our God, and they will reign on the earth.

REVELATION 5:9-10

God understands and speaks every language. He not only knows all of the languages on the earth, He created them. Remember the story of Babel? The people of earth, who all spoke the same language, were getting kind of cocky. They decided to "build...a tower that reaches to the heavens, so that we may make a name for ourselves and not be scattered over the face of the whole earth" (Genesis 11:4).

God was not happy about this so He said in His trinitarian voice, "Come, let us go down and confuse their language so they will not understand each other. So the LORD scattered them from there over all the earth, and they stopped building the city. That is why it was called Babel—because there the LORD confused the language of the whole world" (Genesis 11:7-9). I have often wondered why God did this. He seems more like a builder, constructer, carpenter guy to me than a demolition man. He does hate avarice and pride, though. Maybe Babel is just one in a long line of tales about God demolishing hubris.

As uncomfortable as I am with the destructive aspect of the Babel story, I know God lives and breathes and makes choices I sometimes don't understand. He also redeems things we mess up. In the case of Babel, it took a while. But when we finally get to the Acts of the Apostles, in around A.D. 61, God's Spirit descends upon a large and diverse group of people and helps them understand each other: "All of them were filled with the Holy Spirit and began to speak in other tongues as the Spirit enabled them....A crowd came together in bewilderment, because each one heard them speaking in his own language" (Acts 2:4,6). First God chose to confound. Then graciously He chose to unify language so we could hear and know the gospel.

Sometimes when we pray we feel bewildered. It's easy to freak out that we might not use the "right words" or pray in the "right ways." We have a misconception that our prayers should always be multifaceted, mysterious, and meaningful.

I remember feeling a little uncomfortable about praying with others when I was in high school. I was scared that I wouldn't sound pious or profound. I was worried that there was a secret language of prayer to which I was not privy. At Young Life Youth Group meetings my stomach would cartwheel and my tongue would trip when the leader, Joel, asked me to "open the group time with prayer." One day I confessed to him how nervous I got about praying in front of my peers.

Joel said, "God is more impressed with earnestness of the soul than with a vociferous vocabulary, Sally." He winked at me, impressed with his own alliteration, then continued, "Just say what's on your heart. That'll be the most profound prayer you could ever pray. God is less concerned about logistics and language and more interested in love. But if you're still *really* uncomfortable, remember this little alliterating gem: Practiced prayer in private makes perfect prayer in public. I think that if you cultivate time in your daily life to talk with God, you might feel more at ease when you pray with your friends. Try it! It can't hurt." He slugged me in the arm, walked back to the table, and grabbed a donut.

I took Joel's words to heart and found myself snuggled in my green velvet prayer chair with my Bible almost every day. After a few months, I grew to enjoy my private prayer times, and praying in public didn't feel like speaking in a foreign language any more. Surprisingly enough, the more I prayed alone with God, the simpler my prayers became. Instead of feeling pressure to rise to some exalted spiritual stature, I let it all hang out in everyday words. In fact, my most modest, honest, even embarrassing prayers were the ones that made me feel like I was truly communicating with God. Talking to Him started to feel like talking to a divine friend.

Over time I learned that prayer doesn't have to be plumped with a preponderance of profound pontification. It is best when it comes straight from the heart. I once heard the story of a little girl who was saying the alphabet with her hands folded. When her mother asked her what she was doing, she said, "I'm praying."

The mother asked, "What are you praying?"

Her daughter answered, "I don't know. But I'm just saying all of the letters, and God'll make sense of them all."

Sometimes when we pray, we can feel like that little girl. It's O.K., though, because God accepts—even delights—in our offerings. We don't have to prove *anything* to Him. We're His kids. We should feel embraced rather than embarrassed in His presence. Just as my mom and I are excited and proud to finally be writing the simple Chinese characters for yi, er, and san, so God is impressed with *any* effort we bring to our prayer lives.

The other day when my son Ben came home from school, he had written his name for the first time. The "B" was lumpy and misshapen; the "E" was crooked and floating above the line. The "N" was closed at the bottom and appeared to be a drunken "O." But when I saw the lovely letters, I cried and hugged my son. *He had written his name all by himself…and it was beautiful!* I couldn't have been prouder.

God must feel the same way about our words spoken or written in prayer. In fact, I think He feels a Father's pride about our *entire* lives, our oblations to Him. He's so proud of our offerings.

We needn't worry about our use of language and vocabulary. He makes sense of our babblings because He loves us. In our prayers, we might be limited by language but God isn't. He even promises, in Romans 8:26, that "the Spirit helps us in our weakness. We do not know what we ought to pray for, but the Spirit himself intercedes for us with groans that words cannot express."

Often our best wordings fail when we're trying to share our souls in prayer. God will help us. The Divine Articulator is master and creator of all languages. Yet His favorite is the language of the heart.

*I, who live by words, am wordless when
I turn me to the Word to pray.*[4]

MADELEINE L'ENGLE

Walking the Talk

1. Have you ever learned a foreign language? Take some time to think about or journal that experience.

2. Be straight with God and pray the simple, honest prayer of your heart.

3. If you want to practice your private prayers, think of a plan, write it down, and try to follow it. (Remember to be easy on yourself if you don't exactly stick to it.) Consider praying while you walk, garden, do the dishes, or while

you're on your lunch hour, in a special chair, or on a park bench.

4. If an opportunity presents itself to pray in public, take advantage of it. Don't worry about eloquence; just be yourself.

Lord, thank You that You know the language of my heart. May I be honest with my words as I learn to speak Your native tongue. Amen.

A Circle of Giving

Gifts as Prayer and Prayer as Gifts

*Grace is something you can never get but only
be given. There's no way to earn it or deserve it
or bring it about any more than you can
deserve the taste of raspberries and cream or
earn good looks or bring about your own birth.*

*A good sleep is grace and so are good dreams.
Most tears are grace. The smell of rain is grace.
Somebody loving you is grace.*[1]

FREDERICK BUECHNER

Girl Talk—Margie's Mums

Last Christmas I was sitting in our family room near our
fire and Christmas tree. Cozied in my blanket, I counted the
shiny presents under our tree. They seemed to spill over like
freshly popped champagne. Most of them were for our sons,
Ben and Ayden. Knowing that "it is more blessed to give
than to receive" (Acts 20:35), I decided to take the boys on
a little shopping trip to a local dollar store so they could
each purchase a gift for their daddy.

On the way I remembered a past shopping experience
when Ben and Ayden chose trucks and trains, toy guns and
swords for my husband's birthday. Hoping to do some edu-
cating and preteaching, I asked, "Boys, what do you think
Daddy would be *really* excited to receive for Christmas?"

When the boys recited their personal Christmas lists, I tried a redirect, "When you get a gift for someone, try to think about him. Imagine his hobbies. Think about the things that make him happy. Think of something he'd *really* want, but probably wouldn't buy for himself."

After a short pause, Ben said, "I think I'll get Daddy a tool 'cause he's a carpenter."

I smiled and thought of my friend Margie, who always brings me gifts that show her depth of knowledge about me. She knows that it makes me feel loved when I receive a gift. So inevitably, after Margie visits, I find a wrapped cookbook hiding in my laundry room. Or on my pillow a teacup from one of her trips to London.

During a particularly dark season of my life, Margie showed up on my front door step with yet another gift. In her arms was a basket of nodding yellow mums. "When I saw these at the farmer's market," she said, "God nudged me to bring them to you."

Margie's giving is free and plentiful. Sometimes I feel guilty that she has given me so much. Other times, I worry that I'll do or say something stupid or hurtful and jeopardize her precious friendship. When I have anxiety like this, I try to remind myself that I *have* said and done unseemly things to Margie before, and she didn't desert me. She has been in my life for almost 20 years, and I expect she'll be in it for 20 more, not because of...but in spite of me.

I invited Margie in, and she handed me the flowers. As we shared, we sipped cinnamon tea. I cried and she prayed. "Dear Lord, please cure Sally's chronic back pain. Help her to see that You are a healer even in the midst of pain. Give her hope relating to her desire for a third child...and specifically her longing to have a daughter. Help her to know and feel Your presence and concern for her even as she experiences broken hopes and dreams." I think that Margie interceded on my behalf for over an hour. But being enfolded in her concern seemed to last only a minute.

After Margie prayed for me, she handed me a box tied with a grosgrain ribbon. "This is to remind you that I'll continue to pray for you."

I opened the box to find a charm bracelet. From it hung a cross, a heart, a little girl, and a pair of folded hands. I'm wearing the bracelet now. As I type, its dangling symbols jingle a continuation of the prayer Margie began last summer.

Margie has taught me more about prayer than anyone I know. She and her husband serve hundreds of people each year through their healing ministry. When I'm having a crisis of the body or soul, I call Margie. She comes with holy water and oil to anoint. And often she brings gifts. Through the years I've realized that Margie's prayers are the most precious gifts she's ever given to me.

This time, after she left, I sat in my overstuffed chair, staring at Margie's mums. They looked like miniature suns peeking out of the basket on my dining-room table. In a moment I realized that the mums themselves were part of Margie's prayer for me. They bobbed up and down in the breeze reminding me of the hopes and desires Margie iterated with her gracious gift of prayer.

God Talk—A Gift-Giving God

Every good and perfect gift is from above,
coming down from the Father.

JAMES 1:17

Sometimes gifts are our prayers. Other times prayers themselves are actually the gifts. God is the giver of both. Tangible and intangible gifts flow from Him like lacy snow: free, fresh, and vitalizing. Like Margie, God delights in giving as an expression of His love.

I've already shared some of my negative feelings about the metaphor of Santa as God. There's a flip side to that, though. When I think of God like a jolly St. Nicholas, I see Him robed in red fur. His presence is as full of joy as His belly is full of roundness. Holly encircles His curly, snow-white mane. His lap is broad, velvety, inviting.

Sisters from around the globe gather around His heaven-high balsam fir singing *O Come, All Ye Faithful*. A braided scent of evergreen, pumpkin pie, and cinnamon wafts. God's eyes twinkle like the star on top of the tree. He puts a chubby finger beside a cherry nose and begins reaching into a big, red, bottomless sack.

One after another He pulls out gifts wrapped in chartreuse, violet, and crimson satin. They're all tied with wide, golden bows. The first is large and bumpy. It doesn't fit in a box and requires yards and yards of violet wrapping. A group of God's children greedily rips open corners, sides, and finally the middle of the package exposing the gift: human life.

The next package is crimson and quite warm to the touch. When opened, an enormous blazing ball floats out. The gift: the sun and life-sustaining warmth. God-Santa graciously hands out gift after gift: the ability to work, have babies, and friends...cold water, earth, green grass, grapes, giraffes, golden retrievers...faithfulness, peace, patience.

Then God pauses and wishes special Christmas greetings directed at specific daughters. To Cheri, He says, "Christmas joy to you." He hands her a crimson box. Inside is the gift of creative writing. To Margaret, He says, "Christmas gentleness to you." He hands her a chartreuse box. Inside is the gift of healing. Hannah's next. She's given a violet box. Inside is the gift of laughter. Millions of gifts are doled out. Inside are the ability to paint, a lyric soprano vocal range, wisdom, knowledge of history and science, tolerance, understanding, a heart for the poor.

After the moon and sun have risen and set on many Christmas mornings, God gives one final gift. It's small and wiggly. And it is marked "HANDLE WITH CARE." A woman named Mary is the first to open the gift. She gratefully receives it and reads the attached card. It says, "For God so loved the world that he gave..."

Mary opens the present. It's so lovely, she names it: "God with us, Emmanuel." Then she shares it with the world. In her heart Mary ponders that this gift will bring to bear many more: forgiveness, eternal life, the Holy Spirit...a totally new way of communing with God.

With Mary, we can say, "My soul glorifies the Lord and my spirit rejoices in God my Savior, for he has been mindful of the humble state of his servant" (Luke 1:46-48). With her we can humbly realize the nature of gifts. They're freely given. We do *nothing* to get, earn, or deserve them. They fall on our blackened hearts like purifying snow. All we have to do is meet God at His evergreen and rip into graciousness: receive.

It's so easy to think that faith is something we *do* or even *will*. But it's not. Ephesians 2:8-9 says, "For it is by grace you have been saved, through faith—and this not from yourselves, it is the gift of God—not by works." If we don't recognize God's free endowments, a work-mindedness can plague our entire faith journey. We'll think we have to "be good people" in order to "get to heaven," or "be worthy or special" in order to "be gifted in special ways."

This can be especially damaging in our prayer lives. We may mistakenly believe that prayer is about gritting it out, grinding through motions of intercession, supplication, praise, and repentance.

Thank goodness faith and salvation, special talents and abilities...and *prayer itself* are all free gifts. When we consider prayer as a gift, it's impossible to see it as dull drudgery. Instead it becomes a treasure wrapped in bright, shiny satin. If we open it, God will connect with us in countless, caring conversations. He'll also grant us the gracious desire to pray for others. When we talk to Him, and give the gift of prayer to our friends, we'll widen the circle 'round God's evergreen tree.

The...guardian angel bestows on each infant a unique gift, a gift to which the child will be responsible: a gift of healing; a gift for growing green things; a gift for painting, for cooking, for cleaning; a gift for loving.[2]

MADELEINE L'ENGLE

Walking the Talk

For the wages of sin is death, but the gift of God is eternal life in Christ Jesus our Lord.

ROMANS 6:23

Thanks be to God for his indescribable gift!
2 CORINTHIANS 9:15

1. How do you react when you're given a generous gift? Are you uncomfortable, joyous, grateful? Is it harder for you to give or receive? Why?

2. God offers us many gifts. One that He extends to us is the gift of prayer. How can you accept this gift? Make a list of ways you can change a prayer life of dull drudgery into a celebration where you receive the means and ability to connect with God as a gift.

3. Give a gift to a girlfriend. Make sure to select something that represents your hopes, wishes, and prayers for her.

Father, thank You for all Your good gifts. I especially thank You for the gift of prayer. May I receive it fully instead of trying to force a connection with You. Amen.

Cancer and Compline

The Ministry of Prayer

Pray for each other so that you may be
healed. The prayer of a righteous man
is powerful and effective.
JAMES 5:16

Girl Talk—Margaret's Ministering Prayers

Last June my friend Margaret gave me one of my most memorable, treasured birthday presents: *The Book of Common Prayer*. It was an appropriate gift coming from Margie because, as I mentioned earlier, she's a minister of prayer. I had shared with her that I wanted to incorporate morning and evening prayers from this book into my life. So she inscribed the inside of its black leather cover with the following message: *Dear Sally, I look forward to praying some of these prayers with you as the sun rises and sets on another year of your life. Happy birthday! Love, Margie.*

Almost exactly two months after my birthday, a medical tornado blew into Margaret's life. The twister hit on a seemingly normal Thursday evening. Margie and her family of three had shared dinner, conversation, and bedtime rituals of singing, reading, praying, kissing, and hugging. The house was asleep when, in the middle of the night, Joel, her husband, started shaking in bed. He was facedown in his pillow, and his muscles seemed frozen. Margaret was not sure exactly what was going on. Her husband was completely unresponsive when she pleaded, "Joel, can you hear me? Are you O.K.?"

Frantic, Margaret called 911 and a doctor friend. Via ambulance, Joel was rushed to the nearest hospital. Thankfully he regained consciousness. But results of his MRI showed that Joel's midnight episode was a seizure caused by a tumor in the left temporal lobe of his brain.

The surgeon assured my friends that the tumor was a run-of-the-mill menangioma. He also said, with 99 percent certainty, that it would be benign. Nevertheless, Joel needed surgery to have the tumor removed.

The surgery was scheduled for August 31 (one day before Margie's thirty-fifth birthday). Joel's parents flew in from Brazil. Friends and priests from the community gathered to wait and pray in a special room at the hospital designated "Family and Friends." Joel's sister, Katie, brought decadent brownies and the best coffee I've ever tasted. I, at a loss, brought stacks of colored paper and a Chinese paper folding book. I knew the surgery would be long and figured that playing (along with praying) would help pass the time.

For hours Joel was in the hands of the surgeon while our hands folded birds, baskets, and hearts. At one point during the waiting, Katie told us that she had asked the doc if she could have the tumor for a homeschooling lab project. He said, "I'm not sure about that. The tumor will have to go to pathology. But you can have the brain." We laughed for one of the rare moments of humor that morning.

In the afternoon the surgeon communicated that the tumor had been completely removed. Joel was in recovery. It would be a few hours until even Margie could see her husband. Sensing that there was nothing more I could do, I hugged my dear friend and went home. When I went to sleep that night, I prayed for Margie and Joel. And I anticipated getting good news on the morning of the next day—Margie's birthday.

By evening no news had come. I started to worry. Brushing off my anxiety, I told myself that Margie and her immediate family were probably busy caring for Joel and having a simple yet celebratory party for Margie at the hospital. I didn't want to interrupt the festivities, so I waited to call until after dinner.

"Happy birthday, Margie," I said when she answered her cell phone. "Where are you? How's Joel doing?"

"I'm in my car on the way home. And, Sal, this isn't exactly my *happiest* of birthdays. The surgeon told us this morning that Joel's tumor was worse than they expected. When they opened his skull and saw the tumor, they realized it was a hemangiopericytoma. A rare, aggressive...*cancerous* tumor."

"Oh, Margie," I said. "I am so sorry!" The phone jiggled in my hand, and my voice shook when I asked, "How long until you're home?"

"I'm just about there now," she said with a tired peace in her voice.

"May I come over?" I asked.

"Sure," she said.

I threw on a coat and shoes, grabbed the *Book of Common Prayer* that she'd given me, stopped at Walgreens (to pick up some Ben & Jerry's Chocolate Therapy), and was walking in Margie's door 15 minutes later. She was taking off her jacket and hanging car keys on a hook by the front door. We hugged in the hallway. Both of us trembled with tears.

"I brought you this," I said, holding up the pint of ice cream. "And this," I said, holding up the black prayer book emblazoned with a gold cross. "Can we pray Compline?"

"Yeah, let's," she said. We brought the book and the ice cream into her bedroom. She sat on her side of the bed. I sat on Joel's. The room felt empty without him there.

Since it was my very first time praying Compline, which is a prayer of quietness and reflection, Margie read the part of *The Officiant*. I read the part of *The People*.

The Officiant begins
The Lord Almighty grant us a peaceful night and a perfect end. Amen.

Officiant Our help is in the Name of the Lord:

People The maker of heaven and earth…

Officiant and People

Psalm 91
1 [She] who dwells in the shelter of the Most High…shall say to the Lord,
2 You are my refuge and my stronghold, my God in whom I put my trust…
3 He shall deliver you…
5 You shall not be afraid of any terror by night…
6 Of the plague that stalks in the darkness, nor of the sickness that lays waste at mid-day.

> Be present, O merciful God…so that we who are
> wearied by the changes and chances of this life may
> rest in your eternal changelessness….Amen.

We shed more tears. I felt a soft, comforting presence in the room. It wrapped us like a blanket. I had come to minister to Margaret. But she ended up officiating our prayertime, leading me in my first Compline, ministering grace to me. The rhythm and truth of the words ministered, too.

Compline has been prayed for many years by millions. The strength and beauty it offers is beguiling. That night in Margie and Joel's room, the Compline itself was a minister of grace. All of us were the recipients: two friends sitting on a bed, a husband in the hospital, and anyone needing healing mercy.

The stories of Jesus' healing are particularly poignant to me right now, while I am still in the midst of my own healing. I was not able to reach out and touch the hem of Jesus' garment, but those who loved me touched it for me.[1]

MADELEINE L'ENGLE

God Talk—God, a Minister of Prayer

Like Margie, God is a prayer minister. He gives us ideas and words to pray during times of need. Usually these ideas come out in homegrown, on-the-spot types of prayers:

> Lord, please be with Joel during the surgery. Help
> Margie and her little girl get a good night's sleep

before they go back to the hospital tomorrow.
Father, please bring complete recovery and healing
to Joel. Amen.

Sometimes, though, moments in our lives are so intense
or heartbreaking that we are at a loss for words. At times like
these we can tap into the abundance of written prayers that
God has provided to His people. These prayers can be from
the *Book of Common Prayer* or they can be taken from
poems, songs, creeds, and portions of the Bible. When we're
at a loss for words, God always comes through! (He is the
Word, after all.)

The Book of Common Prayer is new to me because it is
not widely used in my church tradition. But thanks to Margie
and Joel, I'm exploring it, making it part of my regular prayer
patterns. That sweet, little black book contains prayers for
birthdays, bereavement, addictions, protection, guidance,
thanksgiving, agriculture, conflict, country, schools, the sick,
the dying, those having surgery, or having a baby...the list
goes on and on. Come to think of it, if we prayed from the
Book of Common Prayer alone, we'd have enough prayers
for a lifetime!

As we pray using words from others throughout the
course of our lives, the words get embedded into our souls.
They become part of the fabric of our lives. They link us to
believers who have prayed the prayers before us, who pray
them with us now, and who will one day pray them. The
words are enough in themselves or they can serve as
launching pads for more praying. Sometimes the prayer
book evokes homegrown conversations. Other times it leads
us to more written prayers.

When I want to be intimate with the Father, I borrow the words of His Son from Matthew 6: "Our Father in heaven, hallowed be your name, your kingdom come, your will be done on earth as it is in heaven...."

When I've messed up and am too raw to come up with my own words, I recite David's psalm of repentance (Psalm 51): "Have mercy on me, O God, according to your unfailing love....Against you, you only, have I sinned....Wash me, and I will be whiter than snow."

When I doubt, I read the Apostle's Creed aloud as an affirmation of my faith: "I believe in God, the Father Almighty, the Creator of heaven and earth...."

As I mentioned in chapters five and six, I also use songs and poems to communicate with God. When I do, the words of praise and honesty written by strangers become mirrors of my heart.

We expect God to hear and answer our prayers. We expect Him to be a minister of grace through His listening and His responses. But who would have ever thought that He'd minister to us through the actual words of our prayers?

When our wells are dry from the drain of life, God is gracious, giving us words. Sometimes they come directly to our minds and tongues. Other times, He lets us borrow the words of others such as the church fathers, Jesus, King David, writers, poets, and friends. Their words are full of hope and help, faith and courage. God is a prayer minister and so are His words.

Walking the Talk

1. If you don't use *The Book of Common Prayer,* check one out from the library. Maybe you'll like it and decide to

buy a personal copy and incorporate its use into your prayer rituals.

2. Pray a written prayer from *The Book of Common Prayer,* a book of poetry, a songbook, a collection of creeds, or the Bible this week. (Have a friend pray with you, if you'd like.)

3. Do you have a friend who is available to regularly minister to you in prayer? If you don't, ask God to bring this kind of friend to you. As you wait, allow God to minister to you through the words of written prayers.

God, thank You for ancient and modern written prayers that help connect me to You. May the words of those who have gone before me in faith be woven into the textiles of my prayers. Amen.

17

Something in the Way She Moves

Dancing Our Prayers

*Let them praise his name
with dancing.*

PSALM 149:3

Girl Talk—Moondance with Hannah

During our single days, Hannah and I affectionately called ourselves Geek Magnets because we attracted a lot of dates who happened to be geeky. We also had a habit of naming these geeks, based on their most negative characteristics. There was the Fast Eater who never gave eye contact during meals. Instead, nose down, head hovering two inches from his entrée, he shoveled steak and potatoes into his mouth. There was Bad Dancer Man who thought he had *all* the right moves. (He actually looked more like a door swinging on a broken hinge than John Travolta.)

Our list of geeky boyfriends was endless: B.O. Boy, Plant Hanging Guy, Stuck-to-You-like-Glue Guy, and of course the archetypal I'll Call Ya Guy. For years during and after going to Wheaton we laughed, wept, and prayed about our dramas related to men. And for years we freaked out about our ticking biological clocks. Sometimes we wondered which we wanted more, husbands or babies.

Prayers for each other were our sustenance during a long season of singleness. Every talk with God helped renew our hopes of one day being wives and mothers. I vividly remember one conversation in particular. One of the men I was dating had broken my heart because he had more energy for 'Da Bears' (the Chicago Bears, that is) than he did for me. I sat on the cement stoop, which was my front porch at the time, and cried. Over the phone, Hannah prayed: "Lord, please fill Sally's heart with emptiness."

"*Whaaaaat?*" I interrupted between sobs. "Hannah... you're prayin' for the *wrong* thing. 'Fill my heart with *emptiness?*' I'm calling Cheri...at least she'll pray that God will bring a *man* into my life!"

Hannah's resonant voice broke in. "Hold on, Sal. It seems like you might've been trying to *force* this relationship to fit into your heart and your life. Maybe if your heart was completely empty there'd be room for God to fill it with His love and other good things...maybe even a man—in time."

About five years after that prayer, I was greeting Hannah at the front door of the home I now share with Bryan, my husband. When we tried to hug a hello, Hannah and I bounced off each others' hard, round bellies. We were both full with long-awaited first pregnancies. It was an exciting night for us. Our babies were meeting for the first time through layers of uterus, placenta, and flesh. We planned to celebrate their meeting...and our answers to years and years of prayer.

For our celebration we collected every maternity-related film we could find: *She's Having a Baby, Look Who's Talking,* and *Father of the Bride II.* I put out a salty-sweet smorgas-bord including the cliché pickles and ice cream (which we just couldn't stomach). The smell of the pickles, alone, made us gag.

We watched scene after scene of women giving birth. Hannah said, "I think I'd rather go through ten tax audits than pass something *that* big..."

At slow parts in the movies we put the remote controls for the VCR and TV on our bellies and watched them bounce as our babies moved. At one point in the evening Hannah emceed a virtual boxing match between our fetuses:

> Baby Miller with a left jab, followed by a one-two combination. Ooooh! It looks bad. Baby Coleman fights back with a hit to the kidney. Whoa! Looks like... mom has been hit in the kidney, too. Time for a commercial break. We'll be right back after this trip to the potty.

Our movies ended around midnight, but we were still wide awake. Both of us suffered from serious insomnia during all of our pregnancies. Wide-eyed, I rifled through a pile of CDs and settled on a Van Morrison compilation. We took it and my boom box out to the back porch. The autumn evening welcomed us with a needed cool down for our hor-monally heat-ravaged bodies. The moon was as full as Hannah and I were—round, glowing, warm. It was a harvest moon.

Van's crooning bounced off of trees and around my yard. *"It's a marvelous night for a moondance..."* Almost simulta-neously, Hannah and I got off our seats and started to dance. I guess the movement of our babies inspired us to move. It wasn't the prettiest sight. Bellies bounced, bottoms wiggled. Still we felt free and happy and grateful. Our arms swirled and bodies swayed to the swing beat and walking bass line. In the light of the full moon we were rocking our babies to sleep and thanking God for the gift of their lives.

Our dance was the culmination of years of waiting. It was a celebration, an offering of thankfulness for gifts of love and life. The dance was pure joy! The gift of these pregnancies was so immense, literally and figuratively, that words would never be enough to thank God. Of course Hannah and I had thanked Him, verbally, for our pregnancies, together and in solitude. But in the case of a gift so precious, lips, teeth, and tongue—*the* articulators—were not articulate enough.

Our gratitude for the gift of our husbands and first children was beyond words. I think that many times words are just not enough to express our praise, anguish, mourning, or, in this case, exuberance to God. At times like these, body language comes in handy. Moving our hands, arms, feet, and legs was the best way Hannah and I could express our gratitude and love.

And we knew God was out there on the porch, in the moonlight, dancing with us.

God Talk—The Lord of the Dance

Movement is not that common in our culture (except with the work-out craze). We definitely don't see a lot of dancing at the grocery store, in our parks, churches, political institutions, or even on daytime television. (I think that's one of the reasons Ellen DeGeneres has struck such a joyful chord with audiences as she dances a daily prelude to her daytime talk show.) We live in a nation of couch potatoes. Sadly, our only movement is from video games and sitcoms to the comfort of minivans with mini movie theaters in the backseats.

When I help lead worship at my conservative church in Wheaton, I hardly ever see any movement in our congregation. It's sort of disheartening to look out at the body of Christ during a really rambunctious praise chorus and see a bunch of people standing as straight as sticks. Why are we afraid to move? I've visited other churches where movement comes more naturally. People freely raise hands in worship; they're not afraid to move to the music. I like to follow their lead, and hope others will, too.

The Jewish people had a culture alive with dance. On more than one occasion the Bible describes God as the Lord of the Dance. He gives the gift of dance to lighten our lives and bring joy to our hearts. In Exodus, Miriam and other Israeli women bopped in celebration after the Red Sea had opened. In Judges, Jephthah's daughter grooved when her father was victorious in battle. In the psalms, God turns "mourning into dancing" (Psalm 30:11 NASB). In Ecclesiastes, He declares that there is a "time to dance' (Ecclesiastes 3:4). In the New Testament, Salome bumped and jived (Matthew 14:6), and when the prodigal son returned home, there was celebration and dancing (Luke 15:25).

In 1 Samuel, men boogied in celebration of military victories. And in 2 Samuel, God gave King David the urge to shake his booty. Later David is enthroned over the tribes of Israel. He sets up his rule by moving the ark of God to Jerusalem. The ark was a box about four feet long, two-and-a-half feet wide, and two-and-a-half feet deep. It had permanent poles that were used to carry it because no one was allowed to touch it. It housed the Ten Commandments, Aaron's rod, and a jar of manna, among other things. And most importantly, it was the symbol of God's presence. I can just picture the ark being moved to the City of David.

David and all his attendants participated in the ceremonious presentation of the most holy object possessed by the Jews: the ornate ark of God. All of Israel gathers. Trumpets blare and people cheer as if it were an athletic event. But the carriers of the ark are quiet and reverent. Sacrifices of a burning ox and a fatling calf fill the air with the smell of smoke and burning animal flesh. Dignitaries and high-ranking officials, with noses pointed heavenward, line up in a row beside King David. He is dressed in finest raiment—a purple robe embroidered with the finest golden threads, accented with tassels of royal blue. When the ark is presented to him, he disrobes—to everyone's astonishment—and in his undergarments begins to dance.

The dance is joyous! David whirls 'round. He is taken with the ecstasy of being in the presence of God. In the marrow of his bones, David knows that God is dancing beside him. The leaping and jiving continues for minutes. David breaks a sweat but keeps on twirling 'round and 'round. Pure worship!

King Saul's younger daughter, the feisty, self-centered Michal, who was given to David in marriage, sees David dancing. And she "despised him in her heart" (2 Samuel 6:16). Sarcastically Michal confronts him. "How the king of Israel has *distinguished* himself today, disrobing in the sight of the slave girls of his servants as any vulgar fellow would!" (2 Samuel 6:20). She, like many of us, is afraid of dancing.

Her pride and protection of self-image get in the way of a lot of potential fun and praise.

Michal's jealousy doesn't faze David. He doesn't bother to explain his dance to her. He knows that she couldn't possibly understand his zeal for God. And he knows that she wouldn't understand that he removed his royal robes to honor the only true King. David didn't waste one moment trying to explain his dance with the divine. He didn't need an apologist or a swing partner. So, unfortunately, Michal watched motionless from the sidelines. At the end of the passage, we read that Michal had "no children to the day of her death" (2 Samuel 6:23). I don't know if Michal's barrenness was a curse, consequence, or coincidence, but it makes me sad.

I think of the ways Hannah and I were propelled into a prayerful dance by our babies. As I remember us whirling under the full moon, full with our children, I wonder if a pregnancy might've been just what Michal needed to get her groove going with God.

Tis the Gift to Be Simple

'Tis the gift to be simple, 'tis the gift to be free,
'Tis the gift to come down
where we ought to be,
and when we find ourselves
in the place just right,
'twill be in the valley of
love and delight.[1]

SHAKER HYMN

Walking the Talk

1. What is your relationship with movement? Are you comfortable with dancing? When do you give yourself permission to shake your booty?

2. In a safe setting (in your room with the shades drawn, at a wedding reception, in a dance class) dance. How might your movement be a way of communing with God?

3. Consider praying with your posture. The following ideas come from a book by John M. Sweeny titled *Praying with Hands*. Light candles, lay on hands, dance with God, wash feet, assume a prone position, pass the peace, hug, shake hands, gesture the sign of the cross, lift your hands, bless with holy water, anoint with oil.

Lord of the Dance, thanks for my body. I want to use it to bring You glory and gladness. Amen.

18

Don't It Make
My Brown Eyes Blue?

The Prayer of Tears

*And the tear that we shed, though in
secret it rolls, Shall long keep [her]
memory green in our souls.*

CLEMENT CLARKE MOORE

Girl Talk—Emily's Mother in China

One of my dearest friends is a woman I've never met. I don't know her name, the timbre of her voice, or her favorite foods. She may like spicy Sichuan or perhaps she prefers Cantonese stir-fry. She may be boisterous and funny or quiet and demure. She may be a farmer, a teacher, or a stay-at-home mom. She's probably close to my age, but she could be a few years older than I am… or quite a bit younger.

All I definitely know about this woman is that she has black-lacquer hair and almond eyes. She lives in China and is about to give me one of the greatest gifts of my lifetime: a daughter. This faraway friend is the birth mother of a baby girl my husband and I are going to adopt from China this fall.

I've given my friend a name, Meiying, which means beautiful flower in Chinese. I use this name when I pray for her and the baby girl, Emily, that she carried.

Lord, please carry Meiying as she carried Emily.
Give her a healthy postpartum recovery and a
sweet, lasting connection to her daughter. Please
be with Meiying during these tumultuous times for
the family in China. Help her find grace and peace
as she's forced to make the difficult decision of
placing her baby in a location where she'll be
found, placed in a welfare institution, and ultimately adopted by Bryan and me. Let Meiying
know that when she cries, You cry, and that You
care about her as much as she cares about Emily.

For about six months now, I've been preparing paperwork that was just mailed to the China Center for Adoption
Affairs (CCAA) in Bejing. The dossier includes a petition to
adopt an orphan, our birth certificates, copies of passports,
a home study, pictures of our family, and so forth. All of the
documents are officially sealed by the Secretary of State and
the Chinese Consulate. I describe the process of preparing
this package as a gestation of red tape: a paper pregnancy.

During my paper pregnancy, I was struck by a serendipitous occurrence. Almost every time I had to get my stack of
growing papers signed, sealed, or notarized, it was usually
a rainy, hazy, or misty day. Time and again I remember
cloaking the documents inside my jacket to prevent them
from getting wet. Sheltering the bundle felt much like carrying
a little baby. Often I found myself tearing up as I cradled the
valuable paperwork in my arms, under my heart.

I imagined that Emily's birth mother was probably crying
a lot, too. I thought about Meiying and hoped she was
receiving some comfort from her religion. I tried to picture
her in a temple praying and receiving grace. But I didn't

know if Meiying even lived near a religious shrine or if she participated in any kind of religious practice.

I thought about my missionary friend who's currently in China and hoped that among the millions, Meiying might have been exposed to faith in Christ. No matter what her story, I found deep comfort in the image of God collecting Meiying's tears in a bottle (Psalm 56:8 NASB).

Also as I reflect on many rainy trips to the Chinese Consulate in Chicago and to the adoption agency, I realize that Meiying and I were not the only ones crying for Emily...or for China. God was expressing His anguish, too. His tears over lost mothers and daughters of His beloved China symbolically fell in thunderstorms and showers, mists and heavy torrents of rain. The tears were numerous and came throughout the entire adoption process.

In January our paperwork was complete. I put it all in a grand envelope. Noticing that the weather was a predictable gray, I put on my biggest, fluffiest winter parka. Like a mother bear I was prepared to protect the documents that would ultimately link me to my daughter.

On my way to the adoption agency, the sky darkened. I thought about Meiying. I cried tears for her along with tears of personal joy, anticipation, and fear. By the time I pulled onto the long, tree-lined drive leading to our social worker's office, it wasn't raining. It was snowing! Soft, large, white flakes floated from heaven, consecrating the moment as holy. Some of Jesus' famous words came to mind: "Blessed are you who weep now, for you will laugh" (Luke 6:21).

I parked my car and looked heavenward into flecks of freshly falling flakes. I imagined the day I will meet Emily's birth mother. I see her. She is as beautiful as an orchid. She has long black hair and a slender body. I bow to her. She bows in return. Jesus wipes tears from our eyes. Emily takes both of our hands, and we skip down a golden street, laughing in the snow.

Those who sow in tears will reap with songs of joy. He who goes out weeping, carrying seed to sow, will return with songs of joy, carrying sheaves with him.

PSALM 126:5-6

God Talk—When God Cried

Jesus wept.
JOHN 11:35

The shortest verse in the Bible lets us see Jesus sharing our sadness. The verse is: "Jesus wept." It's found in the middle of a story about the death of Lazarus, one of Jesus' closest friends. Upon first reading, it's easy to assume that Jesus' tears are caused by the death of His close buddy, the brother of Mary—the woman who broke the vial of perfume over Jesus' tired feet and washed them with her hair. But if we recreate the story, we might find another reason for Jesus' crying.

Jesus was hanging out with His disciples near the Jordan River, where He'd been baptized by John. Lots of people gathered. They brought picnics and told stories about John and Jesus. Then they started sharing stories about the work God had been doing in their lives. The days were glorious and sunny. The nights sparkled with the light of stars, and the people were warmed by smoky campfires. During those times, many started to believe in Jesus.

One morning, as the mist was melting off the river and the feet of children started to rustle in tents, a man from Bethany in Judea ran into the camp. He was yelling, "Jesus, Jesus...*JEEEEE–SUS!*"

Most of the disciples slept through the shouts. But Peter awoke. Recognizing the man as a Judean, he grabbed his dagger to protect Jesus. Peter had a bad feeling about anyone from Judea. The last time he was there with Jesus, the Jews had tried to stone his Lord.

Jesus rose to greet the man with an embrace. Peter intercepted. "What do you want with my friend?" Peter pushed the stranger to the ground.

Out of breath, the dark-haired man got up, dusted himself off, and said to Jesus, "Lord, the one You love is sick."

"No one here is sick," said Peter.

Jesus got a sorrowful look in His eyes. He immediately knew that the sick man was Lazarus, the brother of Mary and Martha. Jesus loved these people dearly. His heart sank at the news. Slowly and methodically He started to gather kindling on the outskirts of camp for a morning fire. As He did, He remembered staying at the home of his close friends. They had played a physical game similar to charades until the middle of the night.

Jesus could almost hear Lazarus' laugh. It sounded a lot like the braying of a donkey. He remembered refilling the oil lamps several times before dawn broke. He recalled the way their laughter turned into a deep, thoughtful discussion about the conundrum of having a loving God in the midst of a painful world. Jesus missed His Judean friends and was deeply concerned about Lazarus.

With an armful of twigs and brush, Jesus walked toward the dark-haired stranger from Bethany. "This sickness will not end in death," He said. "No, it is for God's glory so that God's Son may be glorified through it."

A look of relief washed over the stranger's face. He stayed for breakfast of smoked fish and unleavened bread, and then he returned to his hometown.

Jesus stayed two more days at the camp. His disciples started getting edgy, worried, and impatient.

John said, "Jesus, I thought You *loved* Lazarus. Why do You tarry so long…when You know he's ill?"

Jesus was silent.

James piped in, "Lord, what are You *waiting* for? Are You scared that the Jews are going to try and stone You again?"

Before Jesus could reply, Peter grabbed his large dagger, wielded and thrust it at an imaginary assailant. "I'll bring weapons to defend You, Lord. No one had better try and stone You this time!"

Then Thomas sneaked up behind Peter and tapped one of his huge shoulders. Peter gasped in fright, dropping the dagger.

Andrew, James, and John busted a gut laughing. John said, "Jesus, You know somethin' we don't know, don't You?"

"Our friend Lazarus has fallen asleep, but I am going there to wake him up."

A confused conversation buzzed about the 12. Then, packing His satchel, Jesus indicated that He was ready to make the trip.

When they arrive at Bethany's town gate, news that Lazarus has been in the tomb four days greets them. Martha runs to Jesus. He embraces her and promises, "I am the resurrection and the life. He who believes in me will live, even though he dies."

Martha looks at Jesus with tired but believing eyes. She knows, however, that her volatile sister, Mary, will surely challenge the tardy Christ.

"Where is Mary?" Jesus asks.

Mary finally shows up at the town gate. She falls at Jesus' feet and with despairing frustration says, "Lord, if You had been here, my brother would not have died." Then she begins to weep, wetting His feet with her tears.

When Jesus sees her crying, He is deeply moved. And He begins to cry, too.

The Jews who had gathered by the gate say, "See how Jesus loved Lazarus!"

But Mary knows in her heart that Jesus' tears really fall because of empathy for *her*. His heart breaks when He sees what Mary has been going through. And He shares in her sadness.

Anytime we experience deep sorrow, like Mary or Meiying, Jesus sees. He realizes that sometimes life is so difficult that we're unable to tell Him about it with words. At times like these, God gives us the gift of tears. The tears wash our hearts and become our prayers. God collects these tears in bottles to show us His concern, His love, His attentiveness. Then, if that isn't enough, He enters into wet and salty communication with us. When we cry, He cries, too.

It's a comforting human experience to cry with a friend during a tough time. The experience becomes holy when we realize that God is crying with us, too. It's also reassuring and hope-giving to know that one day God will be with us and He'll "wipe every tear from [our] eyes. There will be no more death or mourning or crying or pain, for the old order of things [will pass] away" (Revelation 21:4).

When they brought Jesus to the place where his dead friend lay, Jesus wept....To see a man weep is not a comely sight, especially this man whom we want to be stronger and braver than a man, and the impulse is to turn from him...because the sight of real tears...forces us to look to their source where we do not choose to look because where his tears come from, our tears also come from.[1]

FREDERICK BUECHNER

Walking the Talk

It is the wisdom of the crocodiles, that shed tears when they would devour.

FRANCIS BACON

1. Do you consider tears to be a gift or a burden? Consider your feelings about crying. Were you taught that "big girls" don't cry? Do you think you're better off if you keep a "stiff upper lip"? Take some time to think about your perceptions of crying. If you're a free-flowing crier, great! But if tears don't come easily for you, you may want to contemplate the healing grace of tears.

2. Consider a particularly sad season in your life. If you cried a lot during this time, thank God for the tears. Then thank Him for crying with you.

Recently I experienced a special grace of the soft rain of tears....God graciously helped me enter into a holy mourning in my heart on behalf of the Church and a deep tear-filled thanksgiving at God's patience, love, and mercy toward us.[2]

RICHARD J. FOSTER

Father, thank You for the gift of tears that cleanses my darkened heart. Amen.

Tell Me a Story

The Prayer of Reading

> *Story makes us more alive, more human,*
> *more courageous, more loving. Why does*
> *anybody tell a story? It does indeed have*
> *something to do with faith, faith that the*
> *universe has meaning.*[1]

> MADELEINE L'ENGLE

Girl Talk—Katie, Collector of Books

My friend Kate has more books than anyone I know. Hundreds are stacked against a wall in her dining room. Dozens tower by her bed and next to her favorite chair in the sunroom. I often tease Kate that her daughters' rooms are just excuses to have storage for the children's section of her library.

I'm glad that Katie is my friend because I love books *almost* as much as she does.

Katie and I understand each other. We love the smell of books. The feel of them in our hands. The way their colored bindings look like a rainbow on our shelves. We enjoy flipping through pages with our thumbs. When we do we listen for the gentle whisper, "Read me."

Both of our husbands freak out about Master Card bills when they see we've been on-lining at Amazon.com, Chinaberry, or Powell.com. We dismiss them knowing that we help each other find the best places for good deals on good reads. We plan our vacations together around annual book expos (where we can get free novels). And recently we've come up with a scheme to solve Kate's book storage issue, as well as curbing some of my storybook spending sprees.

The plan is to commission my husband, Bryan, to build floor to ceiling, maple, built-in bookshelves for Katie's study. The payment for the shelves? Books, beautiful books! (I can't believe Bryan agreed to it.) Kate's payment plan is to replace all of my tattered paperback versions of *The Brothers K, Crime and Punishment, The Canterbury Tales, Faust, Don Quixote*...with nicely bound hardcover versions. She's also making a mile-long list of children's books that she wants to add to my collection: *The Black Falcon, I Love You the Purplest, When Marian Sang, Chicken Sunday, The Keeping Quilt.*

Bryan doesn't know it yet, but it looks like I'll need some bookshelves of my own soon. It is a good thing I know a great carpenter!

Katie was a literature major at Wheaton. She has probably read more books than anyone I know. Incredibly, she retains information about their major characters, plots, and themes. Yet she plans on hanging a plaque inscribed with "Ancora Imparo" above her new bookcase. It means, "I am still learning." Some believe Michelangelo said these words when he was 87 years old.

Lots of people read, but when Katie reads she *listens* to the stories in her books. She absorbs them. She opens her ears, mind, and heart. She figuratively asks each book she reads what lesson it wants to teach her. And Katie is still learning, growing, and changing. Even though I think she's bright, brilliant and beautiful, she, like Michelangelo, is still on a lifelong journey.

When I was pregnant with my first child, Katie gave me one of her favorite Hans Christian Andersen fairy tale collections. Inside the book's cover, she inscribed:

Dear Sally,

To quote Madeleine [L'Engle], "Children's stories are aware of what many adults have forgotten—that the daily, time-bound world of provable fact is the secondary world, the shadow world, and it is story, painting, song, which give us our glimpses of reality...."

My girls and I love this collection of fairy tales (even the scary parts). We've read it 'til the binding is broken.

I hope you and your children enjoy this book as much as we do.

Love, Kate

God Talk—God and the World's Greatest Stories

Literature helps us pay attention to the world and to the experience of its creatures and to the work of its Creator....In this way it can nourish prayer.[2]

MARK PRYCE

God tells the greatest stories. His Word is full of them. Jesus was full of them. Parables. Epic historical adventures. Love stories. Stories of betrayal, murder, incest, friendship, and faith. God's truth is not limited to stories in the Bible though. The stories of the ancient Greeks, Shakespeare, Dostoyevsky, Jane Austen, C.S. Lewis, Toni Morrison, Anne Lamott, and even Stephen King also hold nuggets of God's wisdom.

Stories that reveal God's attributes have existed in the holy land during days of old and in the ancient ages of Africa, Asia, Greece...*really* they can be found in any culture around the globe. At the same time, God's stories are here in America. They're found in the contemporary and compelling stories of authors such as Lauren Winner, *Girl Meets God,* and Beth Kephart, *Into the Tangle of Friendship.*

Knowing Kate has helped me realize that stories about grace, healing, hope, redemption, truth, and beauty all reflect divine truths. A quick walk down literary lane shows how God can use books to show us how to relate to Him.

Let's start with a Greek myth. Even myths contain truth from God! Remember the story about King Midas? Because of an act of kindness, Midas was rewarded one wish from Dionysus. His wish, of course, was that everything he touched would turn to gold. At first this wish seemed brilliant. Midas would surely become a rich man. But Midas was a rather dim king and soon found that his plan was shortsighted. All of the food and drink he touched turned to gold. And worse yet, when his little daughter ran to give him a hug...she turned to gold.

When we read a myth like this, God teaches us through the story that Midas wanted something that seemed good on the outside, but ended up being harmful. We, too, sometimes ask God for things that are really not so good for us in the long run. Ancient truth. Modern application. Brilliant. Lasting. Faith-filled.

Here's another example. Many have read Margery Williams' *The Velveteen Rabbit*. It's the story of a little boy and his best friend, a stuffed rabbit. The boy loves his toy so much, that he "loves" the pink sateen and velveteen right off. The scruffy bunny helps the boy through a serious illness. But due to germ contamination, it must be incinerated. Without an alternative, the boy gives up his precious bunny. And in a course of magical events, the bunny comes to life, hops into the forest, and then comes to visit the boy who helped him become "Real."

Anyone who has had the pleasure of reading this fairy tale experiences, via the story, the power of love and the recreative gift of letting go. The story is redemptive. It perfectly illustrates that being loved can sometimes be painful, but ultimately love helps us become *more* of who we were truly meant to be. Being loved makes us more real! How lovely!

One more example. *Expecting Adam* is a memoir by Martha Beck. Kate and I just finished reading it for our book club. In the story, Martha, a Harvard doctoral student, discovers that she's pregnant with a son who has Down Syndrome. Through her pregnancy, labor, and mothering of a child who is intellectually simple, Martha learns about true wisdom. Her son ends up teaching Martha things that a higher education never could have. For Kate and me, Martha's story put bones and skin onto Paul's words, "God chose the foolish things of the world to shame the wise" (1 Corinthians 1:27).

A lot of people regard "story" as simple, not for *real* thinkers. But the truths found in story (and other unexpected places, such as Adam of *Expecting Adam*) are more profound and real than any laws of science or mathematical formulas. Story has depth, breadth, and breath. It is alive with truths that help us understand life and live it more richly.

Sometimes when we pray, it seems like God is not responding. We long to hear His voice. It is helpful when we realize that one of the ways He speaks to us is through stories. Over and over, in the Gospels, Jesus says, "He who has ears, let him hear" (see, for instance, Matthew 11:15; Matthew 13:9,43; Mark 4:23; Luke 14:35). One of the ways we can hear is by tuning our ears to the stories of God. His truths will find us if we're listening. They're in the Bible, fairy tales, novels, novellas, myths, legends, and picture books. Reading good books, alone or to my children, is often the most prayerful part of my day. While I'm reading, I'm usually relaxed, open, and *listening*—during moments like these, I can really hear God's voice.

Literature traces in our lives and the life of the world the glory and presence of the living and active God of whom the words of liturgy and Scripture speak.[3]

MARK PRYCE

Walking the Talk

The Universe is made of stories, not atoms.

MURIEL RUKEYSER

1. Make a list of your top-ten favorite books. Write a paragraph explaining why they're on your list. Do you recognize a pattern? A message? A theme?

2. Do you consider your time reading a good book to be sacred? Why or why not?

3. The next time you finish a novel or piece of nonfiction, consider the ways you connected with God because of your reading.

4. Start a book club with a group of friends. Notice how prayerful this can be.

Father, thank You for good friends and good books. Please help me connect with the stories and books You want me to know. Amen.

Working Out Faith

The Discipline of Prayer

*It is only the daily discipline of work at
my desk which frees a book to be born. It
is only the discipline of daily prayer
which allows the freedom of meditation
and contemplation.*[1]

MADELEINE L'ENGLE

Girl Talk—Cheri at Her Desk

Cheri's writing desk is in a quiet corner of her house.
Above it is a blue bulletin board covered with postcards of
famous writers that I've sent her. Pictured in portraits on the
cards are Jane Austen, Toni Morrison, Elizabeth Barrett
Browning, Emily Dickinson, Anne Lamott...all of our
favorites. Scribbled behind the portraits are quotes about
writing from another gem of an author, Madeleine L'Engle.
One reads:

> A book may come...and ask to be written, but it
> takes time and energy and considerable pain to
> give birth to even the most minor of stories. The
> life of the artist is as much a life of discipline as
> that of the physician or the missionary. It makes
> incredibly austere and difficult demands.[2]

Also tacked to Cheri's bulletin board is a picture of me standing by my bright-blue front door. I'm smiling. Beside my head is a wreath inside which a robin has crafted her nest. The nest cradles three round, smooth eggs the color of sky. The photo is nestled among the great writers because that bird and her nest have become a metaphor for Cheri and me of the disciplined life of a writer.

Just as the mother bird wove her nest with twigs, grass, and mud, Cheri weaves stories with words. Just as the pregnant bird laid eggs, Cheri gives birth to ideas. Just as the soft, warm, aviary mama sat on shells, Cheri nurtures and edits articles, manuscripts, and poems. And just as our feathered friend fed hatchlings plump pink worms, Cheri fuels writing with time, effort, energy, devotion, and undying discipline.

Usually, Cheri lives a "normal" life as a stay-at-home mom: doing dishes, changing diapers, and making peanut butter-and-jelly sandwiches. But if an idea falls on her cerebellum like a seed on soil, she pays attention to it. She doesn't rush to the computer greedy for the seed to sprout, however. She gives it time to germinate in her mind.

After a few days, if the idea persists, she scratches down themes and words—in notes to herself. Then she nurses her baby and makes more peanut butter sandwiches for the older kids. If the idea sprouts through dense soil in fresh green persistence, Cheri sets up camp around her writing desk. She brews a pot of hazelnut coffee, grabs a baby quilt and a treasure trove of toys for the boys, and hides a handful of fruit snacks in her pocket just in case she or the kids need an inspirational dose of sugar.

Just like the mother bird planting herself upon a nest, enthroned like a princess, Cheri positions herself in front of her computer. She waits in royal obedience for God to give gracious words. The waiting is not the passive kind; it's active. As novelist Margaret Atwood writes, waiting for ideas is to "Ask what is in the wind/Ask what is sacred."

Cheri asks. And God responds by co-creating with Cheri. He sits beside her keyboard giving creative ideas for the writing and mothering that coexist. He also gives patience, love, and tolerance for her boys...tenacity, wisdom, and strength to rear her paper progeny.

Within the circle of disciplined choices to sit and write, to pay attention to ideas, to submit them to magazines and publishers, to be awake to the wildness and wonder in life, God gives Cheri freedom. It's a freedom to grow in her writing and in her relationship with Him.

Her discipline is not static or driven by legalism or guilt. It changes with each season of life. When baby Sean was born, Cheri put down her pen and basked in the acceptance and publication of her first book. Then she practiced the extremely important discipline of rest, relishing, and rejoicing.

Now that the babe is getting older and beginning the weaning process, Cheri is open to writing ideas again. She's jotting down articles for *Today's Christian Woman, Christianity Today,* and an outline for her new book about post-evangelicalism. She's entering into the grueling process of outlining, drafting, pruning, editing. And she's painstakingly submitting crafted queries addressed to the appropriate editors.

Cheri could have taken the easy way out and ignored her budding ideas. She could have gone to bed early, slept in late, and watched daytime TV. She could have gossiped on the phone for hours each day or eaten bonbons while paging through *Cosmo.* Instead she offered herself willingly, poised and in place at her desk, for God's transforming work. It hasn't all been fun and games. But with each choice to let go of her will and obey God's call on her life to write, Cheri has become surprisingly *freer*. Within the white-picket-fenced boundary of intentional discipline, Cheri runs like an auburn mare with windblown mane, kicking up her hooves in a field of sunlit clover. Because Cheri has taken the time and energy to go to her desk, her writing muscles have been strengthened and her heart and mind have been freed to frolic and play.

The day my robin's babies fledged from the nest, I called Cheri. "They're flying…soaring into the blue!" I exclaimed into the phone. "All four of them made it!"

"I knew they would," Cheri said with calm assurance. Because of her disciplined life, Cheri knew that the mama bird's painful, costly sacrifices would ultimately lead to free flight. She knew that freedom is born from discipline.

For me the disciplines of writing and praying are ever closer and closer together, each a letting go of our own will and an opening up to the power of God's will.[3]

MADELEINE L'ENGLE

God Talk—Jesus

The Disciplines allow us to place ourselves before God so that He can transform us.[4]

RICHARD J. FOSTER

When Jesus chose to place Himself in Bethlehem's cradle, God did a transforming work. One of my favorite passages in the Bible gives us a mysterious and poetic introduction to Jesus' descent into flesh. It begins: "In the beginning was the Word and the Word was with God, and the Word was God. He was with God in the beginning" (John 1:1).

"He was with God in the beginning." What an image! God and His preincarnate Son *together*. I think about this often. It conjures up images of my own sons with their father. I see them playing catch in the yard, sitting side by side on the couch watching NASCAR races, or reading a chapter from *The Chronicles of Narnia* before bed. Intimacy. Shared interests. Physical connections.

I'm sure Jesus and God experienced a heavenly version of this father–son closeness. And I'll bet it was brighter, tighter, truer, and closer than human bonds can ever be. I'm sure the relationship was mutually invigorating and fulfilling. God and Jesus must have laced together the way light fits into the crevices and cracks of darkness.

Picturing their camaraderie makes me wonder how Jesus felt when God asked Him to leave the holy huddle of home. God's request must have seemed insane to Him, as crazy as me asking my unborn son, nestled in utero, to jump into the womb of a Chinese woman and be born in Beijing.

Jesus may have been hesitant. I'm sure He knew the pain involved in birth and life in Palestine: the dangers of birth, fighting famine, being teased, dying. Still, He chose to obey. "Yes, I'll go, Father," He said. Then He walked along the crystal river past the tree of life, gates of pearl, and a city decorated with opals, garnets, pearls, and turquoise. His tears glistened on streets of gold as He obediently said a difficult, painful good-bye.

With a similar yet greatly augmented discipline that places Cheri at her writing desk, Christ placed Himself in a straw-lined feeding trough in an act of obedience. He nursed and toddled. He fished with friends in the village pond, chased pigeons, laughed, kissed a dog's wet nose. In the boundaries of humanity, He transformed Himself. He came near, broke bread with people, laughed at jokes, hugged in tight squeezes, and was hugged.

In obedience and with discipline Jesus got up each day even though His joints ached from sleeping on bumpy ground. He told true stories about fathers and sons, wheat, mustard seeds, and persistent widows. He washed a blind guy's eyes with mud and saliva, restoring vision. Through a simple touch He stopped the bleeding of a woman whose menstruation had lasted for years. His life was painful, difficult, emptying, yet quite full.

Though Jesus gave up a lot, He enjoyed meals by the fire, the feel of sand between His toes, the smell of the ocean, the taste of freshly caught fish, and true friendship. Within the boundaries of a disciplined life, God gave His Son freedom and much joy.

Even more importantly, Jesus' choice to place Himself on the earth and ultimately on the cross produced life everlasting, a seat at the right hand of God, and heavenly glory. His disciplined obedience appeared confining, but it yielded freedom for Jesus and the entire world. His sacrifice and pain resulted in our ability to be completely free. Because He lived within God's boundaries, our lives know no bounds. "So if the Son sets you free, you will be free indeed" (John 8:36).

The Latin word for discipline is "disco." It means to get to know someone. Jesus' life of discipline allowed Him to get to know us more intimately. Likewise, practicing spiritual disciplines, like prayer, allows *us* to know God more intimately.

Living a disciplined life does not mean getting on a spiritual treadmill. It means listening to the voice of God and obeying. It means *knowing* God through the prayer of our lives. That's why prayer is more about a relationship than it is about an isolated act. Sometimes God might ask us to go places that feel foreign or unfriendly or to be willing to die to selfish ways. Other times He might whisper our names and ask us to take a walk with Him, or crack open our Bibles, or pursue one of our gifts, or spend time dreaming.

Each of these activities builds our relationship with God. If we say yes to God's leadings, like Cheri and Jesus did, we put ourselves in a place where God can transform us. The process of growing in prayer may be painful at times, but within its disciplined boundaries, we'll enjoy a closer relationship with God and more freedom than we ever imagined!

Take my life and let it be consecrated, Lord, to Thee.
Take my moments and my days; let them flow in
ceaseless praise.
Take my will, and make it Thine; it shall be no
longer mine.
Take my heart, it is Thine own; it shall be Thy royal
throne.

FRANCES R. HAVERGAL

Walking the Talk

My friend Tom...said that he has longed for
spiritual experiences all his life....He could tell
he'd had a genuine experience when he'd feel a
sense of liberation afterward....This feeling is
something...that ironically, discipline brings.[5]

ANNE LAMOTT

1. What is your relationship with discipline? Do you consider it liberating or limiting? Why? How might you befriend discipline and find freedom through it?

2. Do you sense God nudging you to put yourself in a place where He can bless or touch you? What is that place (a new job, habit, relationship, or experience)? Act on His promptings and see what happens!

Joy is the keynote of all the Disciplines.
The purpose of the Disciplines is liberation
from the stifling slavery to self-interest and fear.
When one's inner spirit is set free from
all that holds it down, that can hardly be
described as dull drudgery.[6]

RICHARD J. FOSTER

Father, thanks for offering me freedom through
boundaries. Help me place myself in safe spots,
relationships, and situations where I can grow
closer to You. Amen.

A Work of Art

Painted Prayers

You will actually see the strokes of the Master creating a work of art. His masterpiece is you—and the colors will be breathtaking.[1]

DEE BRESTIN AND KATHY TROCCOLI

Girl Talk—Lainey's Watercolors

Lainey is an artist. I love going to her showings at various local art galleries. And every summer I happily follow her around the Midwest to various outdoor art shows. Her booth of bold, colorful acrylics stands out as distinctive and unique amid the usual assortment of realistic watercolor landscapes, oil still lifes, and charcoal nudes.

Her style is a cross between Vanessa Bell, Frida Kahlo, and Susan Branch. Her paintings herald verses that outline or are inscribed in everyday items. For instance, in the bowl of a spoon: *It is better to eat soup with someone you love than steak with someone you hate.* Around the border of a quilt: *All things work together for good.* On a mailbox: *Good things come to those who wait.*

Lainey's cheerful masterpieces in lime, periwinkle, red, and bright orange speak of the connections between the daily and the divine. One of my favorites is of a bright-blue coffee cup. Purple steam emanates from the cup. In perfect Lainey fashion, the vapor spells JOY. Also painted under the cup is an artfully imperfect coffee-stain ring on a letter. On the stained paper a poetic paraphrase of Isaiah 61 begins: *Dear Friend, the spirit is around you, lifting your spirits like a good cup of coffee...*

This piece hangs in my writing room. I usually drink a mug of morning java and read Lainey's paraphrased letter each day as I begin to write. I thank God for the Spirit who connects me to the women for whom I write. And I think of Lainey, whose friendship and consistent prayers for me through the years have been spiritual lifters just like that symbolic coffee.

Last year Lainey, five other women, and I shared a Bible study in my home. Each of the studies ended with challenging applications called *Stepping Stones*. One of the studies was about intercessory prayer. The *Stepping Stones* included options to pray a favorite hymn or psalm for a friend, pray written prayers for one another, or fast and pray for someone in need.

One of the applications suggested that we *paint our intercessions* for a girlfriend. Lainey came to the next study with *painted prayers* for all of the women in our group! They were breathtakingly beautiful and truly touching—perfect visual representations of Lainey's hopes and heartfelt desires for each of us. The paintings exhibited verses Lainey had handpicked like wild flowers for each of us. In typical Lainey style, the verses were incorporated in eye-catching colors.

The profound prayers proliferating from Lainey's paintbrush were truly moving. It feels like an indiscretion to describe Lainey's paintings, but for the sake of this chapter, I'll do my best to paint word pictures of a couple of her artistic intercessions.

I vividly remember Margaret's. The painting was divided into two segments. The first was in brown and grayish tones. It looked dusty dry and portrayed a huge husky seed. The seed did not look happy. It was alone, being thrust deep within some soil. The other section was bursting with color. Reds, golds, violets, and greens danced on the canvas creating a windblown rhapsody of flowers in a lush garden setting. A verse in harvest-gold tones framed the entire work: *Unless a kernel of wheat falls to the ground and dies, it remains only a single seed. But if it dies, it produces many seeds* (John 12:24).

Obviously Lainey had prayerfully visualized this painting, picking the perfect colors, images, and verse. She knew that as a new mother, Margaret had been daily thrust into loss like the lonely seed. Lainey, also a new mom, understood the deaths that accompany birth into motherhood. (They are deaths to self, and to quiet, and to date nights…to long showers, to uninterrupted conversations, and to full nights of sleep.)

The painted petition was a way of affirming Margaret's personal sacrifices and asking God to bring life from death by maternity. The blossoming flowers were a picture of beauty bursting forth from dead seeds. Each colorful bloom represented Lainey's intercessory hopes for Margie, Margie's daughter, and *every* mom.

My painting was a collage of hands in many colors. Some of the hands were small: the hands of infants. Others were larger: the hands of adults. Many reached out from the edges of the canvas. And in the center five linked forming a circle.

I knew that the linking hands represented Bryan, Ben, Ayden, the child we are planning to adopt, and me. Inside the circle of hands was another circle of painted words: *You have received a spirit of adoption* (Romans 8:15). I was aware that Lainey had been asking God to give us patience and to protect our daughter until we go to China and bring her home. I also knew that she interceded on behalf of all the world's orphans. Seeing a pictorial representation of these hopes and prayers touched me to the core. Beholding her brushstrokes affirmed our deep desire that God would put the lonely in families (Psalm 68:6).

Webster's Dictionary documents intercession as "prayer, petition, or entreaty in favor of another." This definition is true. But it lacks the dimension, color, and depth the women in my Bible study experienced when we received Lainey's painted petitions. Her compassion, kindness, concern, and love burst forth in bold shapes, colors, textures, and lines that beautifully realized her favorable requests to God on our behalf.

As we took in Lainey's masterpieces, each of us sensed an affirmation of our hearts' deepest desires. We felt understood, loved, vied for. Women with friends like Lainey understand the height, length, and breadth of favorable entreaty. In the same way a Renoir vivifies a scene, prayers from the paintbrush and the heart vivify the word "intercession."

All real art is, in its true sense, religious.[2]

MADELEINE L'ENGLE

God Talk—The Colors of God

*What is a true image? Imagination comes
from "image." The medieval mystics say
that the true image and the true real met
once and for all on the cross.*[3]
MADELEINE L'ENGLE

Jesus is an artist-intercessor just like my friend Lainey. I'm not sure if Christ was an actual artist like Lainey. Maybe He carved wood scraps from His father's carpentry shop into whimsical folk art cats and dogs and sold or bartered them at the local trading post. Perhaps as a child He painted with organic paints made from berries and roots. I can imagine Him proudly presenting Mary with watercolored gifts on her birthday, Mother's Day...

However, I could find no biblical indications of Christ's literal artistry. Still, the Bible is replete with His sensitive, imaginative, artful ways. While Lainey made real her intercessions with painted prayers, Christ realized His intercessions with His life.

Lainey puts hours of painstaking work into her works of art in order to make her ideas real. She chooses just the right shades and techniques to bring her paintings to life. She pours herself, her time, her energy, her talent, her ideas, and her passion into her compositions. Jesus does the same. Lainey's intercessions are worked out on canvas; His are worked out in the choices of His life and ultimately in His death and resurrection.

John, chapter 17, gives an intimate, detailed account of one of Jesus' most inspired intercessory prayers. The prayer took place after the Last Supper and before Jesus was arrested by Roman soldiers. In it He asked for three things: 1) that His friends would be protected after His death, 2) that others would follow the path He started, and 3) that one day all believers would be reunited in a heavenly party. As Jesus interceded, I'm sure His mind was like the mind of an artist, filled with vivid pictures. Just like Lainey, sitting pensively at her easel with one brush in hand and another in her teeth, readied for painting, mind swirling with images, Jesus imagined, too. He saw the color, texture form, and shape of His prayer coming to life.

Jesus' first image was that *His friends, the disciples, would be protected.* I'll bet He pictured His buddies breaking bread, laughing, walking together after His death. Then He saw them missing Him. But when he imagined golden sun shining in their hair and the gentle breeze on their shoulders, He prayed for reminders of His loving touch. He hoped that in hearty hugs, practical jokes, and long-winded reminiscences they'd keep Him alive. That's why He gave them bread and wine and said, "Remember me."

The second intercession was that *others would follow His path.* Like Lainey before a blank canvas, Jesus probably pictured a long line of people following the disciples. They were dressed in native garb: saris, sombreros, kimonos, and kilts. He saw them carrying national flags with honor and pride. Vibrant colors of the people and their wares waved with the rainbow colors of His love. That led Jesus to picture His third prayer, that *we'd all be together, perfected in peace and glory: a family partying in heaven.*

For this part of the prayer, Jesus probably saw Himself as He was before coming to earth, radiant and magnificent, sitting at the right hand of God. He imagined wearing a royal robe. He saw us hanging out with him. Angels were attending. His favorite, Gabriel, whom He called "Gabby" brought Him a triple-decker ice cream cone. It was raspberry fudge, His favorite. Hosts of angels took ice cream orders for all of God's children.

These three intercessions are made real in two final works of art: Jesus' death and resurrection. The day He died, He figuratively painted His prayer for the world. The background was gray. A line of outstretched arms was the focal point. Blood-red accented the shape of a cross. His death was the truest intercession in history. Lainey hung her intercessions on the wall in my family room. Christ, Himself, hung as an intercession. And then Christ rose again—the realization of all His hopes and our salvation.

The artist-intercessor work of His life and death and resurrection are enough: a masterpiece. He doesn't stop there, though. Jesus hands all of us figurative brushes and invites us to complete the work He started: imagining good things for the world and our friends, talking to God about visions of peace and beauty, purification and perfection. He wants us to be co-creators, His apprentices.

We will co-create with colors as distinctive as those found in a pallet of watercolors and with styles as diverse as Monet, Mary Cassatt, and Michelangelo. Some of us will paint our petitions. Others will word our intercessions with tongue and pen. And some will *live* prayers of petition in service to the world, just like Jesus did. As we do, we'll become more than artist-intercessors. We'll become God's works of art! He'll be painted on the canvasses of our lives. "For we are God's workmanship, created in Christ Jesus to do good works" (Ephesians 2:10). Together we'll create quite a gallery displaying the breathtaking colors of God's love.

*The universe is itself a work of art, with God as
the first Artist, the first Poet, and we both
acknowledge our calling by this Maker to be
co-creators, with God, with each other.*[4]

LUCI SHAW

Walking the Talk

*Man is a maker. This is part of what it means to be
in the image of our Creator God. As we learn to
collaborate with Him, He confirms and mightily
blesses the work of our hands.*[5]

LEANNE PAYNE

1. Write a journal entry that expresses your feelings (good or bad) about art.

2. Get a copy of Jody Utal's *Painted Prayers,* or check it out from the library. Read some of her prayers and study the corresponding watercolor paintings. Now make some of your own. Consider painting prayers of intercession for some of your friends.

3. Write a poem or paint a picture that expresses your gratitude for the gift of friends, the gift of Christ, or the gift of art.

4. Take a field trip to a local art gallery. Go alone or with a friend. Let the works of art be the voice of God to you.

Consider ways of being co-creators with God and the artists.

5. When you get a chance, read Jesus' intercessory prayer in John. Consider using it as a model for a time of intercessory praying or painting.

A child playing a game, building a sand castle,
painting a picture, is completely into whatever it is that
he is doing....So, when we wholly concentrate,
like a child in play, or an artist at work, then we
share in the act of creating.[6]

MADELEINE L'ENGLE

Artful Intercessor, thank You for the ways You and my friends wish me well. May Your colorful love inspire me to imagine good things for others. Amen.

When God Says No

Unanswered Answered Prayers

> *I have slowly learned that when God says
> No to my earnest prayer, that No may
> well be the prelude to a wonderful Yes I
> couldn't have begun to predict. If I am to
> enjoy my faith I have to trust the No
> comes from love, not anger.*[1]
>
> MADELEINE L'ENGLE

Girl Talk—Losing Lucy

Sometimes we pray for our friends and God answers with a *yes*. Other times, He gives a different response. For years I've been praying with Lilah. God has answered our prayers with plenteous *yeses*, some *wait-a-whiles*, and a few inexorable *noes*. When Lilah's daughter, Lucy, was fighting against an autoimmune disease, we prayed more fervently than ever before for healing. Our hope was that God would answer our petitions with a *yes*.

Lucy was Lilah's third child and the apple of her eye: a plump cherub with chocolate-brown eyes and soft hair. She looked a lot like her mother and definitely got a sweet disposition through maternal genes. When Lucy was a baby, though, she seemed to get sick more often than Lilah's other two children. About the time that regular bouts of skyrocketing fevers became unmanageable with Tylenol and tepid baths, Lilah sought medical advice.

Unfortunately that first visit to the pediatrician's turned into a medical tsunami. Lucy was diagnosed with a rare disease that left her extremely vulnerable to viruses and bacteria. Infections plagued her, and for the next few months that soon became years, little Lucy spent more time being poked and prodded than playing. When local specialists ran out of ideas to help Lucy, Lilah and her husband had a difficult decision to make: *Should they rent an apartment across the country in order to be near a cutting-edge hospital with state-of-the-art equipment and a stellar staff of specialists?*

Though the expenses were financially and emotionally astronomical, Lilah and Lucy moved across the country, away from a web of supportive family and friends, in order to get treatment and, hopefully, a cure. Almost daily Lilah or her husband e-mailed updates relating to the goings on in their little girl's life: smiles, struggles to eat, spiking fevers, sleepless nights, sweet sad eyes…cookies, chemotherapy, cuddles and coos…tests, treatments, toys…diapers, disappointments, daily joys.

More often than not, my face was drenched with tears as I read their letters. The tears were my prayers. I knew that God was hearing, seeing, and sharing my compassion for Lilah, Lucy, and their family. The moments of petitioning as I read were sacred and holy. My computer screen became an altar. The deepest kinds of prayers I think I've ever prayed happened in the sanctuary of my office.

After a long battle and a litany of prayers like mine, Lucy was released from her daily pain. In her daddy's arms, she breathed her last breath. With a kiss on the forehead and a whispered "I love you," Lilah let her little girl fly to Jesus.

A few months after sweet Lucy's death, I wrote a poem for my friend. It is a circular poem, moving from birth to death to birth:

Water Ungraspable
Life begins and ends, eluding like
Waters broken, shattered in our grasp

We are submerged, swimming and walking
Deeper into living through death
As water slips between the fingers of our
    open hands
Taking and giving, God breathes, and moves,
    and chooses

When I wrote this poem, the last line surprised me. I never really thought of God as someone who would *choose* death. I always regarded Him as the Lord of *life*. I knew He had the power and resources to keep Lucy in life—in *this life* with her mommy. But for reasons I couldn't grasp, He *chose* to keep Lucy "in life" in a different way than we hoped or expected.

Why did it surprise me that God chose to answer our prayers with a *no*? It didn't surprise me when God gave Lucy to Lilah at her birth. But it shocked me when He seemed to take her away. *Did He really take her away? Was Lucy's death His choice?* I don't know. But I do know that God was as sad as Lilah was when her daughter left the world. And I know that even though our prayers for health were answered with an ultimate, heavenly healing, our prayers for an earthly cure were answered with a *no*.

That was really hard to swallow. I got mad at God; I didn't understand why He would give such a lovely gift and then cruelly take it away. In church the Sunday after Lucy died we sang a worship song about the way God gives and takes away…and that no matter what, we can bless His name. I wasn't ready to do that quite yet. But several months after burying her daughter, Lilah was.

She stopped over with her two oldest children and brought a video of Lucy that we tearfully watched. All of us wished to hold and smell the baby freshness we could see on the screen. My son asked, "Where's Lucy, Mama?" We talked about God and heaven. Then we cried harder. We shared a simple lunch of tuna sandwiches and green grapes. While we were tossing the paper plates in the trash, my friend looked at me and said, "I couldn't have gotten through all of this without the goodness and grace of God. The only thing that really seems to help is figuratively falling into His arms."

I hugged Lilah tightly and offered her a napkin for a tear-stained cheek. I admired her reaction to bless God even though He answered her prayers with a *no*. I was amazed that she wasn't looking for reasons or lessons under the stone of catastrophic loss. I was blessed by her acceptance of the incomprehensible. And I was encouraged to see her walking in trust, receiving the gift of faith when fear and sadness seemed overwhelming.

As we stood together in my kitchen, I imagined Lilah falling into the arms of God. When her head hit His strong shoulder, He gripped her in a tight embrace. And I noticed that in His other arm He was holding Lucy….

Because I could not stop for Death,
He kindly stopped for me—
The Carriage held but just Ourselves
And Immortality.

EMILY DICKINSON

Even tragedy can be a means of grace.[2]

FREDERICK BUECHNER

God Talk—God's Give and Take

Love which truly loves enough...say[s] no
instead of the easier yes.[3]

MADELEINE L'ENGLE

Around Jesus' thirty-third birthday He was praying for God to spare His life, just as we prayed for Lucy. His prayer was not said in front of a computer screen though. It was said in the Garden of Gethsemane. It was dusk. The sun slunk behind bare trees, creating ominous shadows. Crickets traded their typical cheery song for a creepy dirge. Rivulets of ruby red sweated onto Jesus' face and brow. When He looked to his closest friends for comfort and reassurance, He noticed them snoring on rocky pillows.

The Father had put Jesus in a precarious, will-shattering position to choose between His will or the cross. Christ knew that His entire human life was leading up to this final moment of liberation. Yet He was afraid to die. Facing a despicable death, Jesus was "deeply distressed and troubled"

(Mark 14:33). He said, "My soul is overwhelmed with sorrow." He fell to the ground and prayed that if possible Abba, Father would reach a holy hand from heaven and take the cup of death from him. His entire life had been a discipline, and for His entire life He made disciples. Couldn't He get a break just this once?

God said no. And then Christ was seized by Roman soldiers, nailed to a cross, and hung 'til He died.

The deaths of Christ and Lucy make me wonder: Does God really answer our most heartfelt requests with yeses? Does He care about our hearts' desires? What does the psalmist mean when he tells us that if we delight ourselves in the Lord, He will give us the desires of our hearts? (Psalm 37:4). If God would truly grant the desires of our hearts when we delighted in Him, then why do we face so many noes in our prayer lives? If delighting means getting yeses, what does "delighting" mean?

Surely, if anyone delighted in God, it was Jesus. And His prayer was answered with one of history's biggest noes. He didn't seem to get the "desires of His heart."

Thinking about the lives of Jesus and Lilah, I realize that delighting in God is not just a one-time thing. It's the journey of a lifetime. It's about knowing Him through His Word, the world, and others. It is about caring about things He cares about: people, peace, goodness, the poor, justice, beauty, the needy, truth, honor, orphans, laughter, and love. It's about talking to Him, listening to Him, and just plain living life with Him.

"Delighting" means holding tightly to things we can hold onto: love, faith, grace, and truth...and letting go of the rest. Both Jesus and Lilah let go. Then they did a freefall into

God. In doing so, they realized that delighting in Him is simultaneously simple and sublime.

When we delight, God *will* give us the desires of our heart. I think He does this in two ways. Sometimes He gives us what we desire. Other times He changes our desires (i.e., gives us new desires that align with His). This doesn't mean that Christ's agonizing death was lessened or that Lilah wasn't heartbreakingly sad about losing Lucy. It just means that as we let go and endure the pain, God will change our desire for a momentary yes into a bigger yes. Sometimes the bigger yes is difficult to understand from our perspective— but it's a *yes*, nonetheless.

Christ offered His life to bring life for many. And Lilah offered up her desire for Lucy's healing and received healing and hope for herself even in the midst of grieving. Both paths were painful, life-altering processes. Both will ultimately lead to more yeses than we can possibly imagine.

Sometimes the thought of altering our desires can be disturbing because it means being open to letting go of things we *really* want. We want to avoid pain at all costs. At times like these, we have to remind ourselves that God cares about us. He knows what's best for us. Nothing tickles Him more than granting our wishes, answering prayers with yeses. At the same time, His noes are for our benefit—even if they're hard to bear or comprehend.

Out of the *no* bringing Christ's death raised the *yes* of resurrection. Beauty often comes from ashes. In Christ, death is extinguished with the breath of life. And all of God's noes will one day be redeemed with one sweeping forever, "Yes!"

God says Yes whenever possible because it is our Maker's pleasure to give us pleasure. We are loved because we are God's and that love is shown most gloriously through Christ's presence in our world and in our lives.[4]

MADELEINE L'ENGLE

Walking the Talk

Events happen under their own steam as random as rain, which means that God is present in them not as their cause but as the one who even in the hardest and most hair-raising of them offers us the possibility of that new life and healing which I believe is what salvation is.[5]

FREDERICK BUECHNER

1. Has God said no to one of your most heartfelt prayers? Why do you think He answered that way? Ask Him to renew the desires of your heart.

2. Do you trust God to give you good things? Why or why not?

3. Memorize Psalm 37:4. Make a list of practical ways that God might be asking you to "delight in Him."

4. Is there a desire of your heart that you are afraid God won't give to you? Talk to a friend about it. Ask her to pray for you. Talk to God about it, too.

Good God, thank You that Your noes are often preludes to wonderful yeses. I want to trust You and accept Your wise answers to my prayers. Amen.

A Drop of Olive Oil

Healing Prayer

> *Healing Prayer is part of the normal Christian
> life....It is simply a normal aspect of what it
> means to live under the reign of God. God cares
> as much about the body as he does the soul, as
> much about the emotions as he does the spirit.
> The redemption that is in Jesus is total,
> involving every aspect of the person—body,
> soul, will, mind, emotions, spirit.*[1]

> RICHARD J. FOSTER

Girl Talk—Margaret's Healing Balm

Recently Margie gave birth to her first child, Charlotte. On a rainy Tuesday Margie brought the baby girl over for my two sons to meet. When they saw her, they launched into twirls, kicks, and spins using the entire space of our family room. Their joy at meeting the little one they'd observed growing in Pastor Margie's tummy manifested kinesthetically.

They didn't even realize they were dancing in their excitement. To Margie and me, their movement was unmistakable. It reminded me that the angels are still dancing in heaven because of Charlotte's arrival. It inspired me to consider movement as an appropriate way of expressing joy. Then it saddened me to realize how out of place it is for adults to leap and dance for joy. Why does our freedom to move get inhibited as adults? Does it hurt too much for us to move? Do we have pain because we move less? Are we too tired to expend energy in such a frivolous manner?

Since giving birth to my boys, I have moved a lot less and with restricted freedom due to chronic and excruciating back pain. Margie had also come that rainy Tuesday to pray for the healing of my pain. While we ate egg-salad sandwiches, the boys continued to rejoice over the glorious meeting. After more playing, we tucked them into their beds and went downstairs.

Margie had mentioned that she'd bring some holy oil for anointing. At first it freaked me out a little bit. I had never been "anointed" with oil. It seemed strange and a little "hocus pocus." But having had an inner tube of burning pain around my hips and lower back for days that turned into months, I was open to *anything* and actually started looking forward to Margie's healing balm.

Doctors, chiropractors, osteopaths, and physical therapists had given me little to no relief, so I was anxiously anticipating "the anointing." I thought about the word "salve" (a soothing remedy for disease). It struck me that "salve" was the root of the word "salvation" (deliverance from danger, difficulty, or the effects of sin). I imagined Margie's caring, familiar hands salving my disease. Simultaneously it felt scary, uncomfortable, humbling, and hopeful.

Charlotte was sleeping in her bouncy seat. We sat down on my couch beside her. Margie is accustomed to praying healing prayers because, as I mentioned earlier, she's a prayer minister at her church. After receiving many healing prayers herself, she learned how to specifically ask for God's help, for His saving graces. She learned how to sing hymns and worship songs as part of her talk with God, and then to wait quietly for His voice. Sometimes she's given images of help and hope to pass on to the one for whom she interceded.

We sat silently side by side on the plaid couch in my sunny yellow living room. Marge pulled the *Book of Common Prayer* out of her big, black bag. Then she rifled around the bag for a few minutes before saying, "Sorry, Sally, it looks like I forgot the holy oil." My heart sank to the wooden floor, dashed and disappointed.

"We'll just have to use some olive oil from your pantry," she said. That's kind of strange, I thought. But I practically skipped to the kitchen, searching for *salv*ation. A few seconds later I walked back to the living room holding the Bertoli EVOO, that I'd used in the pasta the night before. With gentleness, my friend used our everyday oil to make the sign of the cross on my head and in the small of my back. She asked God to help me, to alleviate my pain. After she and Charlotte left, I wrote the following poem.

Welcome Charlotte to the world
Welcome, infant, little girl
Mama holds you for my boys
They dance 'round room as they rejoice

I am Ayden. This is Ben.
Says little man to newfound friend
He recognizes Holy Meeting
As Angels fly, their wings repeating

Joy to the world a child is born
A life has dawned like sun in morn
In fullness of space, pain and time
Life Restored makes Beauty mine

Play and feasting yields sweet rest
The boys find sleep, their heads we've blessed
Mom of Charlotte sits to pray
For healing from my pain this day

Come Lord Jesus to this place
Welcome, Healer, full of Grace
Margie lifts me up to you
And Spirit groans with sounds true

Take my sister in her pain
Bring new life and health again
I welcome Christ in Holy Meeting
Angels fly, their wings repeating

Joy to the world a child is born
A life has dawned like sun in morn
In fullness of space, pain and time
Life restored makes Beauty Thine

My pain was still with me later that evening when I used the olive oil in a chicken dish. It is still with me this morning as I sit in my rocking chair and write. It's definitely not as debilitating as it once was though. My back will probably always be weaker and less flexible than it once was. And my levels of pain will fluctuate from day to day. But God has definitely provided me with a measure of healing grace: a foretaste of ultimate, heavenly healing. His mercies are new every morning. He has made me realize that just as the pain of childbirth brings forth beautiful children, pain often births new beauty and rejoicing.

Because of my degenerative back pain, many things have been born in me. I have compassion for others who live with pain. I "get" them. I feel like we're in a family of shared struggle. I'm also forced to slow down, take my time, not rush through life or I'll cause more damage to my back. Because God has given me some relief, I can also imagine the fullness of His restorative healing that is to come in heaven, where God Himself "will...wipe every tear from their eyes. There will be no more...crying or pain" (Revelation 21:4).

For now, as I live with pain and the hope of ultimate healing, I'm able to pray for others in pain, just like Margie did for me.

Healing prayer is not the "instant fix," nor the bypassing of slow and steady growth. It is that which clears the path and makes such progress possible. It is the appropriation of [power] issuing forth through us quietly, unobtrusively, or, at times, dramatically, to the healing of persons.[2]

LEANNE PAYNE

God Talk—The Hem of God's Garment

Christ empowered and commanded His followers to heal because He knew that all men, in their exterior relationships and within themselves, are broken and separated.[3]

LEANNE PAYNE

Some of my favorite stories in the Bible involve Jesus healing people. I love that He was concerned not only about the souls of His followers, but about their bodies, too. Much like Margie, Jesus used everyday items to touch people with healing grace. Margaret used my extra virgin olive oil. Jesus used His hands, the hem of His garment, oil, words, and mud mixed with spit. Today He also uses doctors, counselors, physical therapists, church elders, friends, and surgeons.

By His love and compassion, commingled with the humility and faith of the sick person, Jesus transforms natural objects and everyday people into supernatural healing elements. In the presence of Christ, even an ordinary, everyday brush with a piece of fabric can become a healing salve.

Having suffered from physical pain, I've read and reread the story of the woman with bleeding in Mark's Gospel, chapter 5, verses 25-34. I'm intrigued by it. Every time I search her story I look for clues, answers about why she was healed. Let's look at her story. And, for our purposes, let's call the bleeding woman "Maddie."

Maddie had been bleeding (probably menstruating) for 12 years. Given the customs of the day, this meant she was ostracized, deemed as "unclean," forbidden to make sacrifices at the synagogue or to be intimate with her husband. Anything or anyone she touched had to be ceremonially washed. If someone sat on a chair or bed she had sat on or slept in, they would be declared unclean. For her personally, the sickness, pain, depression, and disease were isolating enough, but with the added burden of Levitical law, the problem became downright devastating.

Maddie was a social outcast. She probably had few friends, no money, and definitely experienced a strained relationship with her family of origin and husband (if she had one). "She had suffered a great deal under the care of many doctors and had spent all she had, yet instead of getting better she grew worse" (Mark 5:26). Somewhere deep down in her soul, she knew that she had one last chance at recovery. She knew, as crazy as it sounded, that her hope was in the hands of a homeless man named Jesus of Nazareth.

Maddie dreamed about Jesus almost every night. In the dreams He always looked at her with warm, gentle, chocolate-brown eyes of compassion. With Him she didn't need to fill out a medical history or describe the embarrassing medical symptoms as she had many times before. She didn't have to don a dehumanizing open-backed gown or put her feet in stirrups only to be examined by an overworked, unsympathetic practitioner. Jesus intuitively knew the details of her condition.

When Maddie told her mother about the Jesus of her dreams and about His Father who would ultimately heal, redeem, and bring salvation to the world, her mother laughed at the false hopes. With a scoffing tone she said, "This God you speak of is not compassionate or healing. How can He be when He makes my daughter bleed for years on end?"

In the dark of the night Maddie packed a small bag and escaped as silently as snow into the hills. She had heard that Jesus was preaching and healing in a neighboring town and knew she had to get close to Him. On her journey, her mother's voice plagued her. *God is not kind. He brings war, disease, famine, plagues. You heard what He did to the Egyptians, didn't you? He turned their water into blood; He made*

men and animals break out with festering boils....Your
bleeding is His punishment for your sins.

Maddie knew the stories well. Guilt plagued her, and she asked for forgiveness for anything she possibly could have done to anger God. When she did, He gently reassured her with a whisper, "I'm not behind your bleeding and the evil things of the earth. I love misfits. I promise to bring beauty from their brokenness." In her heart, Maddie believed God's words. She knew He would bring new mercies every morning, turn mourning into dancing, and bring life from death.

Nearing the top of a hill overlooking a lake sparkling with rays from the rising sun, Maddie saw a large crowd gathering around Jesus. Even from the distance she knew He was the man in her dreams. She recognized Him because He threw back His head in laughter, just the way He often did in her imaginings. Though Jesus was deeply embedded in the growing crowd that moved like an amoeba, Maddie knew she had to get to Him.

Her heart raced with excitement, fear, and anticipation. She was tired from the night's journey, but adrenaline pulsing through her veins drove her forward. With a tenacity she had caged for over a decade, she made her way through the swarming crowd. Each time she touched someone, a piece of her heart broke because she knew her touch contaminated. Still she pushed forward, hoping God would forgive her.

Sweat gathered under her arms. It dripped down her forehead, chest, and neck. She felt disheveled, embarrassed, unworthy, unclean. But when she caught another glimpse of Jesus, this time a close-up, she knew if she could just get near Him her dreams would come true. A burly man the others were calling Peter hovered near Jesus like a bodyguard. Every time she got close enough to look into Jesus' eyes, Peter wedged his body between them.

Maddie was getting exhausted when unexpectedly she tripped on a tree root. Even though she tried to steady herself, she found herself freefalling straight toward Jesus. On her way to the ground, she grabbed the hem of His garment. "Immediately her bleeding stopped and she felt in her body that she was free from her suffering.

"At once Jesus realized that power had gone out from him. He turned around in the crowd and asked, 'Who touched my clothes?'"

She cowered, afraid that He would chastise her...afraid that her mother's words were true. She imagined that Jesus would tell her He was the one who made her bleed. It was her punishment for being so selfish, so needy, so female. Maddie "fell at his feet and, trembling with fear, told him the whole truth. He said to her, 'Daughter, your faith has healed you. Go in peace and be freed from your suffering.'"

She got up and hugged Jesus. It was the first time in years that she touched someone without the fear of making him unclean. He heartily hugged her in return and knew exactly what she was thinking.

Though her healing in this moment completely cured her physical ailment, Maddie had a journey of recovery that would last the rest of her life. Day after day she replayed the grace she saw in Jesus' eyes. With each reconnection she reminded herself that He was not the source of her sickness—He was the one who made her well, who told her to live a *free* life in His grace.

On this side of heaven I think we experience the limitations of failing bodies, slipped discs, degeneration, cancer, depression, arthritis, and other chronic conditions. Sometimes God chooses to completely, miraculously heal these. He also doles out smaller mercies, new each day, that help us manage the normal deterioration of the human body. Either way, healing is a process. As we go through life, every day we can choose, like Maddie, whether we'll blame our suffering on Christ or whether we will see Him as the healing agent in our lives and in the world.

Going to Jesus for help is an act of humility, honesty, and hopefulness. It's rooted in the realization of need. Something is broken or diseased: a marriage, friendship, a body, heart, family, or career. When we try to touch the hem of Jesus' garment or ask our friends to do it for us when we can't, we open ourselves to a life of hope and healing. If we ask, He'll provide salvific balm, enough for each day. And one heavenly day He'll bring joy, fullness, beauty, and *complete* restoration to our brokenness.

Those of us who've experienced the help and comfort of healing prayers have the responsibility and joy of praying healing prayers for others. Together, we can share in the redemption that comes when we're salved by God's grace. It's a process. "Therefore we do not lose heart. Though outwardly we are wasting away, yet inwardly we are being renewed day by day" (2 Corinthians 4:16).

*And the power of the Lord was present
for him to heal the sick.*

Luke 5:17

Walking the Talk

*The prayer offered in faith will make the sick
person well; the Lord will raise him up.*

JAMES 5:15

1. Is there something for which you desire healing in your
life? Humbly ask a friend to pray for you. (If you're
feeling adventurous, break out the olive oil.)

2. Consider your thoughts about God as healer. Read the
story about the woman with bleeding in Mark 5:25-34.
Record any new thoughts about her story and Jesus' role
in her life.

*Is any one of you sick? He should call the elders of the
church to pray over him and anoint him with oil
in the name of the Lord.*

JAMES 5:14

*Great Physician, thank You for being my Wounded
Healer who knows my pain. I need and ask for Your
redemptive healing touch in my life. Amen.*

The Barnes & Noble Chapel

Study as Prayer

Study is an exacting art.[1]

RICHARD J. FOSTER

Girl Talk—My Brother, the Basketball-Playing Bookworm

At the risk of offending my brother, Rob, I'm including him in a book titled *Girl Talk*. Though he's six feet, five inches tall, played big-ten basketball, and is a high-powered sports attorney in Los Angeles, I've shared some of my sweetest, most meaningful "girl talks" with him. He's truly one of my best friends...and has been for years.

Rob is an enigma who connects with God in ways that surprise, encourage, and inspire me. One of these ways is through study. I like books, and they connect me to God. But I must say that for Rob, study is one of his truest ways of praying. I think Barnes & Noble and his personal home library sometimes feel more like church to him than Bel Aire Presbyterian does.

My brother studies almost everything from the newspaper sports pages to *Car and Driver* magazine, from *Time* to

Thomas Paine's *Common Sense*. Rob has a personal library that includes books you'd expect a pastor/historian/world scholar/theologian or just plain deep thinker to own. The funny thing is that if you saw Rob interacting with the star player of the Lakers at the Staples center, you'd never imagine that when the game is over, he goes home and reads.

It took me a while to understand that through taking in words and ideas—thinking about things, processing them—Rob connects with God. Three specific experiences over our lives as siblings made Rob's communion with God through study apparent to me. The first was more than ten years ago when Rob was at law school. The second was in a monastery in the desert. And the third took place in my family room.

After graduating from the University of Michigan's School of Business, Rob decided to remain in Ann Arbor to get his doctorate in Jurisprudence. I vividly remember an autumn day I spent with him on the campus of U of M's law school. It was one of those perfect days when the smell of books and the beginning of an academic year mingles with the smell of burning leaves. The sky was a cloudless azure blue, and we were enjoying a morning coffee buzz.

Rob took me on a tour of the hallowed law school halls. They were wainscoted in a dark, grainy oak. Every few steps we came upon magnificent stained-glass windows. The fall sunshine streamed through them in golden slants. My brother translated Latin inscriptions on the window panes: "Vox populi, vox dei: The voice of the people is the voice of God. Summum ius summa inurai: The more law, the less justice...."

I imagined Rob learning through the Socratic Method in this place. "The pursuit of knowledge is a noble thing," I said to him with a smile. Pride swelled in my chest and got lodged in my throat until I let it out in a sisterly slug landing on his bicep.

Several years later, Rob graduated magna cum laude: with great honor. He rented an apartment in Santa Monica and started working as a sports agent. For one of my birthdays he flew me out to California and planned a weekend of fun in the sun. On Saturday he packed a delicious picnic of gourmet turkey sandwiches, lemonade, and oatmeal cookies. And in his convertible we drove into the middle of the desert.

"Where are we going?" I asked as I pulled my hair into a ponytail.

"It's a surprise," he said.

A surprise it was! After driving by a multitude of cactus-mile markers, we pulled up to St. Andrew's Abbey in Valyermo. An art festival was being held there. I hungrily took in the color and creativity, as well as the delicious picnic Rob had prepared. Then he took me to his favorite place at St. Andrew's: the bookstore.

For hours we explored works of Thomas Merton, Thomas Aquinas, Chesterton, Lewis, MacDonald. I was overwhelmed by the theological studies and found a place of comfort in a corner of religious children's books. There I discovered one of my new favorite authors, Sandy Eisenberg Sasso. I ended up buying a couple of her books for my boys: *In God's Name* and *God's Paintbrush*. Her colorful, poetic books levitated me from the heaviness of theology. Their simplicity and truthfulness simultaneously seemed to poke fun at and contain the wisdom of the entire bookstore.

Rob bought something with considerably more words. He purchased Thomas Aquinas' *Summa Theologica.* "You're not buying *that* are you?" I asked. My brows were knit in disbelief and doubt. I couldn't even pick the thing up, much less *read* it. It weighed in well over ten pounds.

"I've been looking at this volume for a few years, and I think I'm going to take it home with me today," said Rob, eyeing the book the way I eye a piece of chocolate cake.

At the cashier I cracked open the heavy hardcover and randomly read: "Further, it belongs to the omnipotence of the Divine power to perfect His works, and to manifest Himself by some infinite effect. But no mere creature can be called an infinite effect, since it is finite of its very essence."

I shook my head, looked at my brother, and asked, "You're not going to actually *read* this thing, are you?"

He read it. Cover to cover. He called me with occasional book reports. After polishing off *Summa,* he went on a romp through the curricular requirements for theological students at Fuller Seminary. Sports agent by day...seminary student by night. Rob has become a professor/pastor of sorts. When I see him interact with clients, family, and friends, I'm always amazed to see the ways Rob reconstitutes his deep readings in practical, loving, profoundly wise, yet simple ways.

I'll never forget one such way. It took place in my family room. Rob was on a recruiting trip in Chicago and stopped by to see Bryan, the boys, and me. My brother and I had some wine as we sat by the fire long after everyone else had gone to bed. He had just finished reading Victor Hugo's *Les Misérables* for the third time. As we munched brie and breadsticks, Rob told me the story of the main character, Jean Valjean.

"Valjean stole a loaf of bread," Rob said in a sad, serious baritone. "He was imprisoned and despairing for years…until he met a gracious bishop. Valjean did not respond in kind, however. Instead he stole a bunch of the bishop's silver and fled. When police brought the thief back to the bishop's home for accusation, the holy man handed Valjean two silver candlesticks, saying, 'You forgot these.' The misled police left; Jean Valjean was spared another imprisonment. And the bishop, said, 'I have bought your soul for God.'"

"That's quite a story," I said as I sipped my Merlot.

I put down my glass when I noticed a rare tear in my brother's eye. "That moment changed the course of Jean Valjean's life," he said. "After that he went on to raise an orphan, spare the lives of two men, and extend grace for the rest of his life. The story is one of grace. Really, it's the gospel. Valjean is me," Rob concluded as he stared at my hearth's dwindling flames.

"And me," I replied. Then I added another log to our fire.

As flames flickered and the clock ticked, we sat together in the midst of fresh understanding.

I'm thankful for my brother's years of prayerful study. His readings fill his mind, filter into his heart and life, and then naturally pour out onto others. Rob is much more than my brother and friend; he's a lifelong learner—a rabbi of sorts.

The key to the Discipline of study is not reading many books but experiencing what we do read.[2]

RICHARD J. FOSTER

God Talk—The Student Rabbi

Jesus grew in wisdom and stature,
and in favor with God and men.

LUKE 2:52

Jesus was also a rabbi. Through the Gospels of Matthew, Mark, and John, *"Rabbi"* is one of the preferred names for Jesus. In fact, when Mary Magdalene sees Jesus for the first time after His death and resurrection, she calls Him "Rabboni," which is an affectionate term for "teacher."

Those holding the title of rabbi were teachers or men learned in the laws of Moses during New Testament times. The title means "my master." Though Jesus may not have had access to Barnes & Noble or a local library, He was revered as a rabbi because He was a lifelong learner. Like Rob, Jesus was concerned about knowing the mind of God. His life was about seeing, ordering, and finding the meaning and impact of words and ideas.

The end of Luke 2 recounts the famous story of Jesus as a young boy at the temple. His family went to Jerusalem for the Feast of the Passover. Somehow on the way home, amid the baaing sheep, crying children, singing troubadours, traveling merchants, and overall commotion, Mary and Joseph lose Jesus.

After three days they find Him in the temple *teaching* the local religious leaders. These learned men sit in a holy huddle around the boy Jesus. They scratch bald heads, pull at long, white beards, adjust priestly garments, fidget with prayer beads...and ask unanswerable questions. They're amazed, befuddled, and astonished by the knowledge and wisdom packed in answers from a prepubescent kid.

I always wondered how Jesus knew the answers to their questions, how Jesus could be a rabbi to the rabbis. The obvious answer is that Jesus *is* God. He is the Word, so He knows the words of the Mosaic Law and the depths of its meaning. He holds the wisdom of the world in the palm of His hand. He is the fullness of God. So of course He was a wise, learned, smart, and knowledgeable young man.

That answer feels like a cop-out to me, though. Jesus was also fully human. So He had to learn as He grew. He was born, as are all people, a *tabula rasa,* a blank slate. His baby brain learned language and faces like all babies do. His toddler mind and body wobbled and bobbled before it could walk and talk. As He grew into a boy, He may have learned to write and read or to practice the craft of carpentry. Jesus learned as He grew, just like the other kids in His neighborhood.

So I've wondered about Jesus' wisdom-beyond-years. As a 12-year-old girl I remember questioning how a boy my age could be a teacher to the teachers, especially intimidating old, scripture-quoting, robe-wearing Jewish rabbis. I remember reading Luke 2 over and over, looking for loopholes. I hoped to find God whispering in Jesus' ears or a tiny angelic tutor. Sadly, no supernatural schoolteacher was detectable.

The story was really a "back story" based on verses 41 and 42: "Every year his parents went to Jerusalem for the Feast of the Passover. When he was twelve years old, they went up to the Feast, according to the custom." Because of these verses alone, I had an arsenal of information. Jesus had been near the temple, the rabbis, and their books for more than a decade. Perhaps, I dreamed, His twelfth year was not the first time He got lost in his "Father's house."

Perhaps He stole away from Mary and Joseph when he was five, six, seven... I imagine Jesus buying a piece of smoked tilapia from a street vendor with the one bronze coin in His pocket. Then I see Him slipping behind jugglers, a family with 12 children, and a traveling salesman to get to the temple in Jerusalem. It was a large, elaborate building with high ceilings. Gilded gold embellished arches and altar. Carved wood and flowing fabrics of purple and red adorned her like a bride. Only candles, the sun, and God's presence provided light. When Jesus entered, His breath was taken away. At the same time, He felt as if He was being given the deepest breath of His life.

It was there that God's people came to worship, and there that rabbis and students of the scriptures mingled. I imagine young Jesus noticing a gathering of rabbis and scholars. Perhaps they sat in the shade of a tree in the temple's courtyard or even in an anteroom. Wherever they were, copies of scriptures were surely with them—inspiring rigorous debates on lessons and laws.

When the group of ancient oaks saw the mere sapling of a boy approaching, some rolled their eyes and coughed haughtily. One bright, violet-eyed scholar, however, invited Jesus to join the tribe with a mere twinkle of his eye. Jesus sat beside him, elbow to elbow, robe to robe. I imagine the friendly rabbi's leathery hands unrolling his scrolls, and Jesus becoming bedazzled. Jesus couldn't read. But one sight of the bold slashes and titles of Hebrew set His eyes dancing, His mind whirling. He was drawn to the lines, curves, dashes, and dots of the letters. They seemed to embody something familiar. They looked the way His Father's voice sounded in His soul: bold, beautiful, honest, perfect, mysterious, and true.

I imagine Jesus sitting beside the benevolent, violet-eyed man year after year. He teaches Jesus to read. The law becomes emblazoned into Jesus' mind and heart. He falls in love with the words—the way they sound, the depths of their meaning, the stories they tell, and the ways they connect Him to His Father. After years of scroll reading, Jesus understands that He has not come to abolish the law but to fulfill it (Matthew 5:17).

Jesus *was* a student of God. Like Rob, He noticed things holy and true. Jesus was a lifelong learner, a student-teacher, if you will. Listening to His parables and stories makes it crystal clear that Jesus pondered, considered, and noticed things around Him, whether they were scrolls, people, or situations.

Being immersed in God's truth was the prayer of Jesus' life. It can be our prayer, too, when we realize that words and ideas open our minds to a connection with God. Through time, application, and the sharing of truths with others, the thoughts seep into our hearts and help us commune in prayer with the Rabbi of rabbis.

*Rabbi, we know you are a teacher
who has come from God.*

JOHN 3:2

Walking the Talk

When we study a book of the Bible we are seeking to be controlled by the intent of the author. We are determined to

hear what he is saying, not what we would like him to
say.... This process revolutionizes our life.[3]

RICHARD J. FOSTER

1. If time and resources allow, plan a two- to three-day retreat for study. Bring your Bible, a Bible dictionary, and other books you may want to use. Consider inviting a friend and partaking in a feast of ideas during mealtimes.

2. Memorize a verse or passage of Scripture. Think about key words, and look them up in your resources.

3. Read a spiritual classic such as A.W. Tozer's *The Pursuit of God,* C.S. Lewis' *Mere Christianity,* or Dorothy Sayers' *The Mind of the Maker.*

4. Read a book of the Bible straight through. Take notes. Consider its meaning and impact on your life.

5. Reread one of your favorite novels prayerfully, openly, even studiously. Notice what passages move or impact you. Ask Jesus to teach you something as you read.

Study produces joy. Like any novice we will find
it hard work in the beginning. But the greater our
proficiency the greater our joy.[4]

RICHARD J. FOSTER

Rabbi, thank You for my mind, scholarly resources,
and the joy that comes from learning. May I be a
lifelong learner and prayer. Amen.

In the California Sunshine

Prayer as Jumping for Joy

Let all thy joys be as the month of May,
And all thy days be as a marriage day.

FRANCIS QUARLES
To a Bride

Girl Talk—My Cheerleader Sister-in-Law-to-Be

If I could give my brother's fiancée a name, it would be Joy. But her mom chose Kristin. Kristin is one of the most joyful women I know. You almost have to meet her to experience her enormous "joy quotient." It radiates out of her like beams from the sun. It effervesces to overflowing like bubbles in a bath. She's the definition of ebullient, bubbly, giddy, elated.

Writer that I am, if I were to punctuate her sentences, I'd end them all with exclamation points! She does this automatically, but not on paper. She uses her body. Honestly, Kristin ends many of her declarations with a cheerleading, spread-eagle jump known as a "herkie." Please allow me to illustrate, using our first meeting as an example.

Setting: a cafe on a cliff in Malibu Beach. Rob and I are drinking lattes when Kristin walks in to meet me. She has just finished a shift at Cedars-Sinai, where she's a caring, compassionate, competent pediatric intern. Though she hasn't had sleep for more than 24 hours, she looks as fresh and beautiful as a Cover Girl model.

Rob (gets up from table and walks toward pretty young woman with flowing blond locks): Sal, this is my fiancée, Kristin.

Sally (stands and extends a hand to Kristin): Hi...

Kristin (blows off my handshake, and goes in for a warm, hearty hug): It's sooooooo nice to meet you! (Breaks hug; does a herkie.) Rob has told me so much about you! (Does another herkie!)

Sally: I'm thrilled to meet you, as well. Rob has told me so much about you, too!

Kristin: How do you like Malibu? Isn't it beautiful?! *(Does mini-herkie.)*

Sally: I don't think I've ever seen so many golden retrievers in one place in my life.

...And the coast up here is breathtaking...

Kristin: This is one of my *favorite* places on the planet! *(Huge herkie!)*

My friends back at home laugh when I tell them about Kristin's herkies. They're not laughing at Kristin, though... they're laughing at me. Apparently when I was in my twenties, I used to punctuate with herkies, too!

When I'm around Kristin, talk to her on the phone, or correspond via snail or e-mail, her joyousness inevitably rubs off on me. It's like walking through a field of wildflowers and inadvertently getting pollen on your sleeves and socks. Around her I'm pollinated with flecks of joy!

Recently I got an e-mail from Kristin regarding her upcoming nuptials. The comment in the subject line was enough to set me into a tailspin. It read: RE: Measurements for Bridesmaid Dress. I broke into a cold sweat and immediately started craving one of the brownies sitting on my kitchen counter (that I'd successfully avoided eating for three days).

When asked to stand in the wedding, I figured that a dress size would be necessary. But measurements? *Measurements!* Nearing forty, experiencing the *fullness* of life after carrying the pregnancies of two large sons and now coming close to peri-menopause, the last thing I want to do is *measure* my growing hips and diminishing chest.

I read on. Kristin, in fact, needed my measurements the *next* day (no time for a crash diet). True to form, she gleefully suggested that I turn the measuring ceremony into a "date night" with Bryan: candles, champagne, something lacy, and a...tape measure! *She's got to be joking!* I thought. A familiar tune from *Sesame Street* rang in my head: One of these things just doesn't belong here...

Over dinner that night I read the e-mail to Bry, and I added, "The only thing that would make our night *more* romantic would be adding my scale to the list of blissful, sensual accoutrements." Bryan laughed. Then he said, "Didn't you just finish writing an article about being beautiful because you're loved...not loved because you're beautiful?"

I blushed. "Yep."

Bry hugged me, and whispered in my ear, "You're going to be gorgeous at the wedding, Sal. I can't wait to walk down the aisle with you...again."

I felt a flicker of joy in my heart because of Bryan's love. And I was freed to smile at the way Kristin sees every moment in life as an opportunity for playful fun.

The next day when I collected my mail, I experienced another burst of bliss from Kristin. It was in the form of her wedding "Save the Date" notice. It wasn't the typical postcard. It was a handmade booklet laced together with a bright yellow ribbon tied into a bow. The pages were sunny, too. Delightfully they lauded: *Rob and Kristin's Love Story, The Schedule of Nuptial Events, Fun Things to do in Newport Beach, Info on Getting Here & There, Places to Stay,* and *A Yellow Ribbon Welcome!* I imagined herkies of joy punctuating each page.

As I read, I felt warm, tingly, and expectant inside like a bottle of champagne with a loose cork. With each page flip, a lemony profusion emitted. I wondered if it was the scent of happiness. I thought about all of the ways Kristin takes life's lemons and makes them into lemonade. She has such a delightful way of squeezing out every succulent drop of life in a joyous embrace. I see it in the way she loves her patients, her daily duties, my family, her friends, wedding activities, God, and my brother. The other day on the phone she said, "I love Rob so much that I have to tell him every five minutes." I believe it! Her zest for living and loving is so abounding it bubbles over.

As saccharinely sweet as her young love is, I'm thankful for the measure of joy she's bringing to my brother's life. And I am overjoyed that as she becomes my sister-in-love, her joy will pour over me, too. I can't wait to stand beside Kristin in ecstatic endorsement of her marriage to Rob. Who knows, I may even do a herkie!

*The whole man is to drink joy from
the fountain of joy.*[1]

C.S. LEWIS

God Talk—Jesus, Our Joy

The joy of the LORD is your strength.
NEHEMIAH 8:10

God is as overflowing with joy as my sister-in-law-to-be is. In the very beginning, He creates. I imagine God's voice is booming, proud, full, and frolicking as He says, "It is good!" I can almost hear His thundering laughter as a centipede tickles His hairy arm and the vivid oranges, reds, and greens of the toucan tickle His eyes.

He delights in creation. The psalmist tells us that He "wraps himself in light as with a garment; he stretches out the heavens like a tent....He makes the clouds his chariot and rides on the wings of the wind" (Psalm 104:2-3). When I picture this I see majesty and splendor. I also imagine God as childlike and playful like Kristin. I see Him playing "dress up" with sunbeams the way my boys dress up as firemen and police chiefs. I see Him beaming with joy as He fluffs His heavenly tent. I'm sure He has as much fun with it as the boys and I do when we make a tent out of quilts, chairs, tables, and sleeping bags. Tents are fun and campy. There's nothing stoic about a campsite. And there's nothing stoic about God. It's sad that we picture God in the temple more often than we picture Him "riding on the wings of the wind." The Bible says that He's a camper. He's free and flying like Aladdin on a magic carpet ride. His holy garments rustle in the breeze; His gorgeous mane of white hair and beard blow in a gale of glorious wind. He smells of fresh air. He beams with the joyous glory of creation. The corners of His eyes are deeply etched with wrinkles from eons of gregarious grins. Sometimes I think God is more likely to invite His children to wrestle than to read or write.

God radiates in effervescent gaiety when He connects with us, His children, in any way—scholarly or playful. Picture Him in Jesus' parables of the lost sheep, the lost coin, and the prodigal son (Luke 15). At the end of each of these stories, when the lost is found, God rejoices to beat the band. He hoists a stinky, bleating sheep onto muscular broad shoulders. He goes home. He calls friends and neighbors and invites them to a celebratory picnic. He pours lemonade, sets out the croquet, and tells hearty jokes.

When the lost coin is found, He sings a bass solo with a heavenly choir of angels. The timbre of His voice is deep, bright, and blasting with beauty. His facial expressions and gestures are raised in pure joy.

At the return of the prodigal son, in an undignified fashion God hikes up royal robes and runs. His steps are broad and bold. His gait is simultaneously that of an old man and a toddler. When God meets His long-lost son He throws heavy, happy arms around him. Then He douses a dusty head with years of saved-up kisses.

God is a God of rejoicing. Over 400 biblical references

contain the words "joy," "joyous," "joyful," or "rejoice." Not only is God full of joy, but He invites us to rejoice. One of His most poignant invitations to join in the joy came in the birth announcement of His Son via an angel: "I bring you good news of great joy that will be for all the people. Today in the town of David a Savior has been born to you; he is Christ the Lord" (Luke 2:10-11).

John responded to God's invitation to rejoice when He first met Jesus. Luke describes this response in the story of pregnant Mary's visit to her cousin Elizabeth. Before Mary even got into the house for a seat and a much-needed drink of water, Elizabeth said, "Blessed are you among women, and blessed is the child you will bear!...As soon as the sound of your greeting reached my ears, the baby in my womb leaped for joy" (Luke 1:42-44). John leapt for joy at the coming of Christ! Then he spent the rest of his life inviting us to share in his joy.

God, John the Baptist, and Kristin all know that Jesus is the source of our joy. He is, in fact, our joy. I can just see God, the proud Father, expectant for the birth of His Son. Like daddies of today, He waited in anticipation, prayer, agony, and excitement. The night Jesus was born I don't doubt that heaven was as relieved and happy as hospital waiting rooms when fathers announce that moms and babies are alive and well.

I imagine God handing out bright-blue bubble gum cigars to attending angels. Heaven must have been bursting with chewy fun and frivolity when Jesus was born. Cartwheels! Herkies! Fireworks! Champagne! Streamers and confetti!

This should be the spirit of our prayer lives—not dull, dark drudgery that comes with restlessly gripping a bunch of beads and vainly repeating a mantra or forcing a quiet time.

Prayer is not about a coerced conversation with God or a required spiritual motion. It's about embracing life with Christ the way John did and Kristin does. It's about celebrating Christ's birth and life. Rejoicing in our relationship with Him, talking to Him from a place of desire, devotion, excitement, and contentment.

It's about painting, singing, dancing, even breathing our prayers. It's about feeling God's touch in the breeze, hearing His laughter in the wind. Prayer is receiving His grace in a note from a friend or a book of the Bible. It's about talking to God with joy and meaning and a light heart. And jumping for joy when He answers our prayers with a *Yes!* or even doing a herkie as a way of punctuating our prayers.

I used to wonder what Nehemiah meant when he wrote that, "the joy of the LORD is your strength." In light of my relationship with Kristin, I think it means that as God's joy bubbles over in abundance, it becomes our joy. And when we don't have the strength to muster up a will to do what we want to do, God gives us the gift of joy and tells us to walk with Him in freedom and delightful desire.

As we begin to pray because we want to, not because we ought to, we realize that our most joy-filled prayer experiences are just tiny foretastes of the communion we'll have with God in heaven. Anytime we think or feel that we're truly connecting with God in our prayers—seeing Him, knowing Him—we must realize that it's just a shadow of the deep joy we'll experience when we see Him face to face. The more we connect with Him in the fullness of conversation, the more deeply we'll want to pray. Joy is contagious and multiplies just like families do!

All joy...emphasizes our pilgrim status;
always reminds, beckons, awakens desire.
Our best havings are wantings.[2]

C.S. LEWIS

Walking the Talk

Then will I go to the altar of God, to God,
my joy and my delight.

PSALM 43:4

1. Is it easy for you to see the joyful side of God? Try to imagine Him as full of joy.

2. When was the last time you did a herkie? What joyful expressions do you exhibit? Can you imagine them as part of your prayer life? Embrace the joy even if it makes you feel a little childish!

Neither should we think of the Spiritual Disciplines
as some dull drudgery aimed at exterminating
laughter from the face of the earth. Joy is the keynote
of all the Disciplines....Singing, dancing,
even shouting characterize the Disciplines
of the spiritual life.[3]

RICHARD J. FOSTER

Father, You are my joy! May I bubble over with more and more of You! Amen!

Daily Doldrums or Daily Dance?

Ordinary Life as Prayer

*Rejoice always; pray without ceasing;
in everything give thanks.*

1 THESSALONIANS 5:16-17 NASB

Girl Talk—Mom in the Mundane Marvelous

*God intends the Disciplines of the spiritual life to be
for ordinary human beings: people who have jobs,
who care for children, who must wash dishes and
mow lawns. In fact, the Disciplines are best
exercised in the midst of our daily activities.*

*Outwardly you will be performing the regular
duties of your day, but inwardly you will be in
prayer and adoration, song and worship. In a new
way, cause every task of the day to be a sacred ministry to the Lord. However mundane your duties,
they are for you a sacrament.[1]*

RICHARD J. FOSTER

One of my friends has been more instrumental than all
the others in teaching me how to talk with God. This friend

happens to be my mom. She's one of the most deeply spiritual women I know. Her connection to God is as long, high, deep, and wide as the Grand Canyon. Though I'm tempted to compare her to Madeleine L'Engle, Mother Teresa, or Anne Graham Lotz, the fact is that my mom is, happily, an everyday gal. She lives a quite normal, family-centered, practical life.

Her spirituality rises up to heaven like a buoyant red helium balloon only because her feet are firmly planted in dark, earthy, Illinois clay. A nurse by trade and a care-giving maternal type at heart, Carol was born in the small town of Mankato, Minnesota. She married my dad, a teacher, at a young age and moved with him to a suburb on Lake Michigan's north shore. There they had my brother, Rob, and me. For years Mom spent her days doing domestic-related activities: stirring pots of homemade marinara, planting zucchini and sunflowers in our backyard garden, helping glue toothpicks into bridges for science fair projects.

On the outside she looks like the typical "desperate housewife." But anyone close enough to see her heart knows that Carol isn't desperate, she is dedicated. Dedicated to her husband, children, community, and, most importantly, to God.

Her dedication (and consecration) is not about playing a pious part or acting out a showy spirituality. It is not formal, proper, or segregated from the muck and mess of daily living. It is deep, organic, homespun, and true. It is woven into the fabric of her life. She loves God and commits everything she does to Him.

Carol is a cleaning queen. She cranks up Michael Card's albums as she scrubs toilets and scours tubs. While doing so one day she was overcome by a particular instrumental piece titled "Meditation." The music (and Spirit of God through it) caused her to weep. Tears poured from wells in her eyes in warm lines that ran down her cheeks, then dappled her light-blue sweatshirt.

Though she favors Martha over Mary in temperament, Mom made a pact with God that every time she heard "Meditation," she'd stop and bow. What a perfect metaphor for her life. She goes about her days. She listens to God. And she responds by consecrating herself to Him as a holy offering.

Whether she's in the overstuffed blue chair doing a Bible study, ironing one of my dad's shirts, having coffee with a friend, throwing a dinner party, playing with her grandsons, serving at her church, Mom is *with* God; she is in communion with Him. She's the one who introduced me to the idea of communicating with Him while waiting in a traffic jam, baking a raspberry pie, taking in a sunset, and even during walks. For years we've shared "ABC Prayer Walks." We put on our Nikes and hit the prairie path. As we walk, we pray aloud using the letters of the alphabet as prompts. Each letter reminds us of a person, place, or circumstance that calls for prayer or praise.

Lately I've come to realize that Mom not only finds little snatches of time during her busy days to connect with God, she also regards her *entire* day—every breath in it—as communion with Him. She's communing as she stitches a quilt, takes a shower, sings a lullaby, unloads the dishwasher, reads her favorite book. Her prayerful connection to God is unbroken.

That's why whenever I *really* need someone to pray for me, she's often the first person I call. Mom's prayers, in person or over the phone, are filled with compassion and realness. They're honest and true because they burst out of her daily connection to the divine. Like daisies in the spring, her prayers break forth from the rich soil of her life. The soil has become fertile because my mom has consecrated it, set it apart, as belonging to God. Her life is a prayer.

[God] wants us to relate to Him with our whole beings, with the totality of our personalities. But many of us intellectualize Christianity. We approach it much as we would a crossword puzzle in The New York Times. *We are quite satisfied if all the little squares are filled....However, a vital relationship with the Lord is based on more than head knowledge! He wants to get inside our hearts too—our psyches, our personas.*[2]

DON WYRTZEN

God Talk—God, the Daily Divine

It's easy to picture holy ground as shiny, cold, deeply veined marble in a temple, synagogue, or church building. And it's easy to picture priests or holy people as men dressed in red or purple robes with large jewel-encrusted crosses hanging over their navels. These images are not necessarily God's pictures of a holy priesthood of believers. His priests drive minivans, get lost in the desert, stutter, and run home-based businesses out of their family rooms.

Three months after the Israelites left Egypt, they came to the Desert of Sinai (Exodus 19). They set up camp in front of its famous mountain. God called Moses to meet Him at the summit. Moses, weary from the already-long journey, combed sand out of his hair with arthritic fingers and wiped a dusty face with an even dustier tunic. Then with worn walking stick in hand, he made the hike toward the Heavenly One.

God surprised Moses with His words. First He told Moses to remind the people of Israel about the provision at the Red Sea: "You yourselves have seen what I did to Egypt, and how I carried you on eagles' wings and brought you to myself. Now if you obey me fully and keep my covenant, then out of all nations you will be my treasured possession" (Exodus 19:4-5).

Moses shook a weary, wind-blown head. He scratched his eyes and pictured his people: barefoot, carrying all of their earthly possessions on their backs, worn down and beaten from the abrasive desert wind. They looked like a band of homeless bag people. They *were* a bunch of bag people. Even the milk of nursing women had dried up months ago. And the strength of the bravest men had been deadened by exhaustion. *A treasured possession?* Moses thought. *What kind of treasure can we possibly be?*

Before Moses could ask any more questions, God continued, "'Although the whole earth is mine, you will be for me a kingdom of priests and a holy nation.' These are the words you are to speak to the Israelites."

Kingdom of priests? Holy nation? God has sounded a little crazy before, but this time He must be completely off His

rocker! Maybe He should take a better look at us? It's obvious
that "priests" are the furthest things from who we are. By day,
we swear, complain, and curse. By night, men and women
trade tents, looking for comfort in strange bedfellows. Even
our children, in desperation, steal food and homemade toys
from each other.

I can just hear Moses: "I'm exasperated and exhausted,
God. Surely, the people will laugh at me when I tell them
that you want us to be a 'kingdom of priests and a holy
nation.'" God didn't change His mind. By the time Moses
reached the desert valley, he knew in his heavy heart he
had to share the news with the elders. When he did, instead
of the knee-slapping laughter he expected, he got this
response, "We will do everything the LORD has said."

Flabbergasted, Moses tapped into his secret stash of dried
apricots. He sat in the shade of his tent for an hour, resting,
chewing one sweet fruit after the next, and chuckling to himself. Fortified for the trek back up the mountain, he was
ready to take the people's reply to God. He bounded up the
craggy path. This time God met him within a cloud almost
as dense as dirt. Struggling to inhale, Moses heard God say,
"Go to the people and *consecrate* them."

Moses let out an affirmative, "WHOAAAAA!" Then God
blew away in a gale of glorious wind; and Moses smiled the
whole way down the mountian. He even sat down and slid
like a child on some of Sinai's smooth spots. He was going
to consecrate his people. The ragamuffin Israelites in the
dusty desert were about to become *a kingdom of priest and*
a holy nation.

We are a lot like the Israelites. On our own we don't pos-
sess extraordinary wealth, wisdom, beauty, talents, powers
or prowess. But because we're God's children, we can be

consecrated, set aside for Him. By following the lead of my mom and Israel, we can bow to God and our daily doldrums can become a dance with the Divine.

When consecrated to God, our lives are transformed into something transcendent. Our humanity becomes holy. Dinner tables become altars for communions. Play dates at the park become sanctuaries of salvation. Phone calls become confessionals. No matter how dusty our daily lives are, with God they can shine like the stars in the heavens.

There is a God right here in the thick of our day-by-day lives who may not be writing messages about himself in the stars but in one way or another is trying to get messages through our blindness as we move around here knee-deep in the fragrant muck and misery and marvel of the world.[3]

FREDERICK BUECHNER

Walking the Talk

Work done as unto the Lord can be a form of prayer.[4]

LEANNE PAYNE

1. Do you see your life as segregated into *holy* and *human* or *daily* and *divine*? How can God's presence sanctify every second of your waking and sleeping, dusting and dancing, resting and rejoicing?

2. Make a list of activities in your life that "can't possibly be prayerful." (You might include doing the dishes, making love, taking a walk, or sitting quietly by the fire.) Ask yourself why these activities are on your list. Then dispel any lies.

Everybody prays whether he thinks of it as praying or not. The odd silence you fall into when something very beautiful is happening or something very good or very bad. The ah-h-h-h! that sometimes floats up out of you as out of a Fourth of July crowd when the sky-rocket bursts over the water. The stammer of pain at somebody else's pain.… These are all prayers in their way.[5]

FREDERICK BUECHNER

God, You give meaning to my madness. Thank You for elevating my everyday life to a sacred, prayerful place. Amen.

Patchwork, Stitching in the Ditch, and Cozying Up

Quilted Prayers

*What with rearin' a family, and tendin' to
a home, and all my chores—that quilt
was a long time in the frame.
The story of my life is pieced into it.
All my joys and all my sorrows.*[1]

LINCOLN COUNTY, WEST VIRGINIA, QUILTER

Girl Talk—Cheri's Stitches

A few years ago Cheri and I took a quilting class together. I recall that it was a patchwork class. My memories are more about moments we shared than the contents of the class. (Though as I write terms such as strip-piecing, stitching-in-the-ditch, and free-form quilting come to mind.) I remember sitting in rocking chairs side by side in a huge barn that had been converted into a sewing store. Amish quilts in bold, vibrant colors and geometric perfection hung from rafters as material inspiration.

I can still smell the starchy fabric and the dampness of the barn. It was so much fun to select our fabrics, cut them into squares, and reconstruct them into works of art. Cheri and I didn't finish our quilts. And our husbands never could understand why we would cut up perfectly good calico only to sew it back together again.

Cheri ignored the "incomplete" of our first class and the jabbing from our men. She launched into a quilting frenzy. Since the class she has made dozens of baby quilts as shower gifts for new moms in our circle of friends. She stitched an elaborate Christmas quilt for her mother. Cheri put together an unbelievably beautiful memorial quilt honoring the life and death of her sister Sue's daughter. Cheri mailed squares of muslin to her sister's friends and to family members. They embroidered or embellished their blocks with fabric paints or markers and returned them. Cheri pieced them together with a cotton sashing, put on a backing, and bound it. When she presented the stitched memorial to Sue, it provided a quilted celebration of life and honored the passing of a cherished child.

Currently Cheri is creating a quilt out of fabrics from old family clothing. Included in the throw are scraps from outfits her children wore home from the hospital, a patch of her husband's jeans, part of her daughters' outgrown dress-up clothes, and a swatch from her deceased grandmother's dress. On the back of a quilt she stitched the following poem:

> Pieces from her old prom dress, scraps from
>   his best tie
> Quilted in with love and grace and thread
>   the shade of sky
> Memories and moments are embodied in
>   this craft
> With hope that memoirs of their lives for us
>   will last.

Cheri gives away a piece of herself in her quilts. As a symbol of the love, energy, and thought she puts into each of her handcrafted gifts, she sews a tag in the back corner of the creations. It reads: Quilted with love from Cheri.

When the book about faith and friendship we coauthored was released, I followed her lead and sent a quilted gift of love to her. Nestled in a deep box I packed a mug, a box of chamomile tea, and an embroidered quilt. On ten of its squares bright pink and green thread spelled our book's section headings: *Passages of Grace, Shared Steps, The Way in Us...A Different Dance, The Circular Journey.* Cheri told me later that she lit a fire, brewed a cup of tea, and snuggled up in the warm memories of our friendship.

Patchwork? Ah, no! It was memory, imagination, history, biography, joy, sorrow, philosophy, religion, romance, realism, life, love, and death; and over all, like a halo, the love of the artist for her work and the soul's longing for earthly immortality.[2]

ELIZA CALVERT HALL

God Talk—God's Patchwork

You can give the same kind o' pieces to two persons, and one'll make a "nine-patch" and one'll make a "wild-goose chase," and there'll be two quilts made out o' the same kind o' pieces, and jest as different as they can be. And that is

jest the way with livin'. The Lord sends us the
pieces, but we can cut 'em out and put 'em
together pretty much to suit ourselves, and there's
a heap more in the cuttin' out and the sewin'
than there is in the caliker [calico]....[3]

ELIZA CALVERT HALL

God is a quilter of sorts. He takes all the bits and pieces of our lives—praises, confessions, requests, tears, secrets, songs, words, joys—and carefully crafts them into a work of art. Sometimes from our vantage point all we see are dark squares or errant stitches. But in His kind hands—through the years—the quilts of our lives become masterpieces made with divine love.

I can picture God sitting in an enormous rocking chair on heaven's porch. Several quilts are airing out over His picket fence. Another one is held in a frame waiting for finishing details. A crazy quilt is in God's artful hands, being graced by an attentive detail-oriented eye. It's the quilt of your life. It embodies all of your prayers; all your connections with God. Sunflowers bend over his shoulder, trying to get a glimpse of the quilted story. A tall glass of lemonade sweats on a bent-willow table beside God's rocker. He's too busy and focused on crafting to take a sweet swig.

The piece He holds is a pink floral representing the day you were born—the first time you cried out to Him. Around its edges God adds a pale yellow blanket stitch. He remembers your little fingers and toes thinking, "before I formed you in the womb I knew you" (Jeremiah 1:5). His heart warms with remembrance.

The next piece is striped silk, navy and gold. You recognize it as your father's favorite tie—the one he was wearing when he was buried. God wipes a large, lopsided tear from His cheek as two more dapple the edge of your crazy quilt. He chooses a split stitch for around the tie. His hands seem too large to be as agile as they are. The stitches fly though. He rocks while reciting the words of Psalm 116:15: "Precious in the sight of the LORD is the death of his saints."

A cardinal wings into the porch. It lights on God's shoulder and sings a melody from one of Bach's chorales. God grins and moves to another section of your quilt. The piece He picks up is white lace from your wedding dress. *At the beginning the Creator "made them male and female" ...and the two will become one flesh...therefore what God has joined together, let man not separate.* He remembers your wedding day fondly and tacks the lace to the quilt top with hundreds of rose-colored French knots.

Next He proceeds to three pieces of pastel cotton: one blue on blue plaid, one orange-and-yellow stripe, and a pink-and-green polka dot. They represent your two sons and daughter. He uses a braid edging to weave them into the quilted prayer of your life. "Behold, children are a gift of the LORD, the fruit of the womb is a reward" He murmurs (Psalm 127:3).

Last, you recognize a triangle scrap. It looks like the new red wool suit you wore to a recent job interview. God lovingly attaches it with a heavy black herringbone. You wonder if that's a fortuitous sign. This time, *you* think of a verse—Psalm 90:17: "May the favor of the Lord our God rest upon us; establish the work of our hands for us—yes, establish the work of our hands." The verse is your prayer and God stitches it, with ardor, into the crazy quilt of your life.

When He's done with the red triangle, God stands up, fluffs your quilt in the wind, and hangs it over the porch railing. He picks up the lemonade and sits to drink. The cool, sweet-sour mixture is refreshing. God examines your quilt. He chuckles to Himself at the way it's turning out: a beautiful surprise, a truly cocreated work.

You chose brown and blue when He planned on purple and green. You picked velvet when He anticipated 100 percent cotton. You wanted to grab the embroidery needle time and again. But with the trust of a child, you relented. He added fern, trellis, stem, blanket, brick, ermine, and feather stitches to perfectly complete the work.

The blanket is becoming incredibly lovely: a perfect representation of your growing relationship with God. The darks and lights contrast; textures play like kids at the park. Pieces are gathered together in a holy shroud. God knows that many more swatches are yet to be added to the crazy quilt of your life…and so do you. As your quilt flutters in the wind, both of you anticipate the journey to come, and together agree that "he who began a good work in you will carry it on to completion" (Philippians 1:6).

Walking the Talk

She never knew how her great idea came to her.
Sometimes she thought she must have dreamed
it.…Her nimble old fingers reached out longingly
to turn her dream into reality.…She put the

thimble on her knotted, hard finger with the
solemnity of a priestess performing a rite.[4]

DOROTHY CANFIELD FISHER

1. Imagine the quilt of your life. What does it look like? Write a detailed description of it.

2. Spend some time thanking God for cocreating the quilt of your life.

3. Perhaps you may want to take a quilting class and feel the metaphor of coquilting with your own fingertips.

God, thank You for taking the prayerful squares of my life and sewing them into a quilted masterpiece. Amen.

Epilogue

*Now two of the disciples were going to
Emmaus. As they talked Jesus came up and
walked along with them; but they didn't
recognize him. As they approached the
village, the men urged him, "Stay with us."
So he went in at the table with them,
he took bread and broke it. Then their eyes
were opened and they recognized him.*

LUKE 24 paraphrase

The sun is rising on another summer day in the Midwest.
The house is kept in quiet while my children are still asleep.
A blue heron wings her mighty way past my window en
route to her enormous nest in the weeping willow by our
pond.

I've just read the biblical story about two friends on the
road to Emmaus. Their sandals emancipate dust on a Pales-
tinian path as they talk about a gentle man who died three
days earlier by crucifixion. While they walk and talk, another
sojourner joins them. He listens to their tales for many-a-
mile, and then he ends up staying with them for supper in
a hillside village.

At the dinner table, the vagabond stranger breaks a
freshly baked loaf of bread releasing a yeasty aroma. He
doles out warm, white hunks, and the two friends have an
epiphany. They realize that the man with whom they've
been walking is none other than *Jesus of Nazareth*, the man
of whom they spoke.

You, dear reader, and I are a lot like those friends. This book has been our "road to Emmaus." As we've had some *girl talk,* God has joined us for the journey.

Along the way, we've shared stories about friends and stories about God. Often I gave God human characteristics. I in no way intended to minimize God. My hope was to bring Him close, just as Jesus was next to the men on the road to Emmaus, in order for us to get a glimpse of God's grandeur. By seeing Almighty God as a friend, a fellow traveler, I hope He has become more accessible, available, and ultimately enlarged.

I also hope that as a result of taking this journey, the place of prayer is broadened in your life.

May you and your friends find Jesus in unexpected places. And as you walk together, quilt, study, dance, talk on the phone, sing, paint pictures, read e-mails, laugh, do laundry, go to work, take vacations, and take in sunsets, may you remember that *all of life is prayer.* Amen.

Notes

Why Did Prayer Feel Like Drudgery?

1. Oswald Chambers, *My Utmost for His Highest* (Grand Rapids, MI: Discovery House Publishers, 1992), May 26.

Chapter 1—The Heart of Hospitality

1. Madeleine L'Engle and Luci Shaw, *Friends for the Journey* (Ann Arbor, MI: Servant Publications, 1997), p. 117.
2. Ibid., p. 125.

Chapter 2—Known…and Loved Nonetheless

1. Madeleine L'Engle and Luci Shaw, *Friends for the Journey* (Ann Arbor, MI: Servant Publications, 1997), p. 162.
2. Madeleine L'Engle, *The Rock That Is Higher: Story as Truth* (Colorado Springs: Shaw Books, 2002), p. 201.

Chapter 3—Long-Distance Friendship?

1. C.S. Lewis, *The Letters of C.S. Lewis to Arthur Greeves* (New York: Collier/Macmillan, 1986), p. 477.
2. Sally Miller and Cheri Mueller, *Walk with Me: A Journey of Faith & Friendship* (Grand Haven, MI: FaithWalk Publishing, 2005).
3. Frederick Buechner, *Godric* (San Francisco: Harper & Row, 1984), p. 34.

Chapter 4—Bread vs. Stone; Fish vs. Snake

1. C.S. Lewis, *Perelandra* (New York: Macmillan, 1965), p. 200.
2. Oswald Chambers, *My Utmost for His Highest* (Grand Rapids, MI: Discovery House Publishers: 1992), December 17.
3. C.S. Lewis, *Mere Christianity* (New York: Macmillan, 1952), p. 81.

Chapter 5—This Song's for You

1. Walter Savage Lander, quoted in Kenneth W. Osbeck, *101 Hymn Stories* (Grand Rapids, MI: Kregel Publications, 1982), p. 1x.

Chapter 6—A Woman of Words

1. Susan Goldsmith Wooldridge, *poemcrazy* (New York: Three Rivers Press), p. xii.
2. Leanne Payne, *Listening Prayer* (Grand Rapids, MI: Baker Books, 1994), p. 23.

3. Robert E. Harrist, *The Embodied Image* (Italy: The Art Museum, Princeton University, 2001), p. XVII.
4. Trent C. Butler, ed., *Holman Bible Dictionary* (Nashville: Holman Bible Publishers, 1991), p. 516.
5. Payne, *Listening Prayer*, p. 23.
6. Madeleine L'Engle, *The Rock That Is Higher* (Colorado Springs: Shaw Books, 2002), p. 217.

Chapter 7—It's O.K. to Play
1. Lucy Maud Montgomery, *Anne of Green Gables* (New York: Random House, 1988).
2. Richard J. Foster, *Prayer: Finding the Heart's True Home* (New York: Harper-SanFrancisco, 1992), p. xii.

Chapter 8—Telling It Like It Is
1. Michael Card, *Immanuel* (Nashville: Thomas Nelson Publishers, 1990), p. 92.
2. Ibid., p. 92.

Chapter 10—Empty to Fill
1. Richard J. Foster, *Celebration of Discipline: The Path to Spiritual Growth* (San Francisco: Harper & Row Publishers, 1978), pp. 48-49.
2. C.H. Spurgeon, quoted in *Celebration of Discipline*, p. 48.
3. Foster, *Celebration*, p. 42.

Chapter 11—I Think I'll Go for a Walk Outside
1. Brennan Manning, *The Ragamuffin Gospel* (Sisters, OR: Multnomah Publishers, 2000), p. 91.
2. Ibid., p. 90.

Chapter 12—Turkeys, Yule Logs, Christmas Trees, and Stars
1. Madeleine L'Engle and Luci Shaw, *Friends for the Journey* (Ann Arbor, MI: Servant Publications Books, 1997), p. 125.
2. Donna Farley, *Seasons of Grace: Reflections on the Orthodox Church Year* (Ben Lomond, CA: Conciliar Press, 2002), p. 12.
3. Dennis J. Billy, *There Is a Season: Living the Liturgical Year* (Liguori, MO: Liguori Publications, 2001), p. xii.
4. Brennan Manning, *The Ragamuffin Gospel* (Sisters, OR: Multnomah Publishers, 2000), p. 95.
5. Madeleine L'Engle, *The Rock That Is Higher: Story as Truth* (Colorado Springs: Shaw Books, 2002), p. 179.
6. Farley, *Seasons of Grace*, pp. 11-12.

Chapter 13—Zimbabwe, China, Afghanistan, and Brazil
1. C. Herbert Woolston, "Jesus Loves the Little Children."
2. Philip Yancey, *What's So Amazing about Grace?* (Grand Rapids, MI: Zondervan Publishing House, 1997), p. 155.
3. Teresa Gustafson, "Love Is a Blanket," *Lutheran Woman Today*, November 1990.

Chapter 14—Love in Any Language
1. Peter Hessler, *River Town: Two Years on the Yangtze* (New York: Perennial, 2001), p. 73.
2. Ibid., p. 64.
3. C.S. Lewis, *The Letters of C.S. Lewis to Arthur Greeves* (New York: Collier/ Macmillan, 1986), p. 96.
4. Madeleine L'Engle, *The Weather of the Heart* (Colorado Springs: Shaw Books, 2001), p. 52.

Chapter 15—A Circle of Giving
1. Frederick Buechner, *Wishful Thinking: A Theological ABC* (New York: Harper & Row, 1973), pp. 33-34.
2. Madeleine L'Engle, *The Summer of the Great-Grandmother* (New York: Harper-Collins, 1974), p. 140.

Chapter 16—Cancer and Compline
1. Madeleine L'Engle, *The Rock That Is Higher: Story as Truth* (Colorado Springs: Shaw Books, 2002), p. 132.

Chapter 17—Something in the Way She Moves
1. Sydney Carter, "Lord of the Dance," ©1963, Stainer & Bell Ltd., London, c/o Hope Publishing, Carol Stream, IL. Used by permission.

Chapter 18—Don't It Make My Brown Eyes Blue?
1. Frederick Buechner, *Telling the Truth: The Gospel as Tragedy, Comedy, & Fairy Tale* (San Francisco: Harper & Row, 1977), pp. 36-37.
2. Richard J. Foster, *Prayer: Finding the Heart's True Home* (New York: Harper-SanFrancisco, 1992), p. 38.

Chapter 19—Tell Me a Story
1. Madeleine L'Engle, *The Rock That Is Higher: Story as Truth* (Colorado Springs: Shaw Books, 2002), p. 220.
2. Mark Pryce, *Literary Companion to the Lectionary* (Minneapolis: Fortress Press, 2002), p. xi.
3. Ibid., p. xii.

Chapter 20—Working Out Faith
1. Madeleine L'Engle, *The Rock That Is Higher: Story as Truth* (Colorado Springs: Shaw Books, 2002), p. 284.
2. Carole F. Chase, comp., *Madeleine L'Engle Herself* (Colorado Springs: Shaw Books, 2001), p. 18.
3. Madeleine L'Engle, *The Rock That Is Higher: Story as Truth* (Colorado Springs: Shaw Books, 2002), p. 217.
4. Richard J. Foster, *Celebration of Discipline: The Path to Spiritual Growth* (San Francisco: Harper & Row Publishers, 1978), p. 6.

5. Ann Lamott, *Bird by Bird: Some Instructions on Writing and Life* (New York: Anchor Books, 1994), p. 233.
6. Foster, *Celebration of Discipline,* p.2.

Chapter 21—A Work of Art
1. Dee Brestin and Kathy Troccoli, *The Colors of His Love* (Nashville: W Publishing Group, 2002), p. 101.
2. Madeleine L'Engle, *A Circle of Quiet* (San Francisco: Harper & Row, 1972), p. 49.
3. Ibid., p. 16.
4. Madeleine L'Engle and Luci Shaw, *Friends for the Journey* (Ann Arbor, MI: Servant Publications, 1997), p. 19.
5. Leanne Payne, *The Healing Presence* (Grand Rapids, MI: Baker Books, 1995), p. 75.
6. Madeleine L'Engle, *A Circle of Quiet,* pp. 10-11.

Chapter 22—When God Says No
1. Madeleine L'Engle, *The Rock That Is Higher: Story as Truth* (Colorado Springs: Shaw Books, 2002), pp. 181-82.
2. Frederick Buechner, *Telling Secrets* (San Francisco: HarperCollins, 1991), p. 32.
3. Madeleine L'Engle, *Bright Evening Star: Mystery of the Incarnation* (Colorado Springs: Shaw Books, 1997), p. 142.
4. L'Engle, *The Rock,* p. 182.
5. Frederick Buechner, *Telling Secrets,* pp. 31-32.

Chapter 23—A Drop of Olive Oil
1. Richard J. Foster, *Prayer: Finding the Heart's True Home* (New York: HarperSanFrancisco, 1992), p. 203.
2. Leanne Payne, *The Healing Presence* (Grand Rapids, MI: Baker Books, 1995), p. 63.
3. Ibid., p. 37.

Chapter 24—The Barnes & Noble Chapel
1. Richard J. Foster, *Celebration of Discipline: The Path to Spiritual Growth* (San Francisco: Harper & Row Publishers, 1978), p. 58.
2. Ibid., p. 63.
3. Ibid., p. 60.
4. Ibid., p. 66.

Chapter 25—In the California Sunshine
1. C.S. Lewis, *The Weight of Glory and Other Addresses* (New York: Macmillan, 1980), p. 354.
2. C.S. Lewis, *Letters: C.S. Lewis/Don Giovanni Calabria* (Ann Arbor, MI: Servant Books, 1988), p. 359.
3. Richard J. Foster, *Celebration of Discipline: The Path to Spiritual Growth* (San Francisco: Harper & Row Publishers, 1978), p. 2.

Chapter 26—Daily Doldrums or Daily Dance?

1. Richard J. Foster, *Celebration of Discipline: The Path to Spiritual Growth* (San Francisco: Harper & Row Publishers, 1978), p. 49.
2. Don Wyrtzen, *A Musician Looks at the Psalms* (Grand Rapids, MI: Daybreak Books, 1988), p. 11.
3. Frederick Buechner, *The Magnificent Defeat* (San Francisco: Harper & Row, 1985).
4. Leanne Payne, *The Healing Presence* (Grand Rapids, MI: Baker Books, 1995), p. 200.
5. Frederick Buechner, *Wishful Thinking: A Theological ABC* (New York: Harper & Row, 1973), pp. 70-71.

Chapter 27—Patchwork, Stitching in the Ditch, and Cozying Up

1. Alfred Allen Lewis, *The Mountain Artisans Quilting Book* (New York: Macmillan, 1973).
2. Eliza Calvert Hall, *Aunt Jane of Kentucky* (Boston: Little, Brown, 1907).
3. Ibid.
4. Dorothy Canfield Fisher, "The Bedquilt," from *A Harvest of Stories* (New York: Harcourt Brace, 1956).

Other Great Books Presented by Harvest House Publishers

Discovering Your Divine Assignment
Robin Chaddock
God loves you and has a purpose for your life—a "divine assignment" that will fulfill your deepest longings. Drawing on her years of experience as a life coach and her deep Christian faith, Robin Chaddock helps you discover your primary passion and greatest strength. Informative, easy-to-read chapters include fun and challenging questions to help you explore your beliefs, your passions, and your goals. With these valuable insights, you can encourage yourself and your family, assist others, and fulfill your God-given purpose.

Overcoming the 7 Obstacles to Spiritual Growth
Dwight Carlson
Have you taken a detour in your spiritual journey? If we're honest, we all get stuck from time to time. When you're not feeling a hundred percent satisfied with your Christian walk, what can you do? Dwight Carlson, bestselling author of *Overcoming Hurts and Anger,* explores the obstacles that hinder faith and reveals the steps you can take to overcome them and grow in the Lord. You *can* look forward to an extraordinary life as you embrace the challenges and triumphs of living in Christ!

Small Changes for a Better Life
Elizabeth George
Don't settle for okay when best is in sight! Are you *almost* happy? Is success just out of reach? Whether your life needs minor adjustments or a major overhaul, bestselling author Elizabeth George helps you pinpoint problem areas and then reveals the small changes you can make to transform your life into one of greater achievement, contentment, and joy. Using the Bible as a guide, Elizabeth explores how to find fulfillment and excel in your relationships, friendships, spiritual life, and more. Seek—and achieve!—God's best for your life.

The Prayer That Changes Everything®
Stormie Omartian
Bestselling author Stormie Omartian shares how powerful prayer can be in your life. Packed with personal stories, biblical truths, and practical principles about offering praise in the middle of difficulties, sorrow, fear, and yes, abundance and joy, *The Prayer That Changes Everything* encourages you to "live each day making praise your reaction and not a last resort."

7 Simple Steps to a Healthier You
Dawn Hall
The creator of the Busy People's Cookbooks and author of *Comfort Food for Your Soul,* Dawn offers inspiration, guidance, and surefire steps to help you embrace a healthy lifestyle. On this journey to physical, emotional, and spiritual fitness, you'll discover advice for handling weight issues, hectic schedules, and unhealthy behaviors. You'll also find the exercise and food plans that will work best for you and promote success.

Conversations with Jesus
Calvin Miller
A celebrated teacher, poet, and preacher, Calvin offers a creative, intimate way for you to listen to Christ. Daily devotions include a Bible verse, a prayer, and Jesus' response presented in first-person narrative. This fresh look at Jesus reveals His love for God, humankind, and His followers. You'll experience a faith that is richer, deeper, and more real as you ask God, "What do you want me to do today?"